MILESTONES
IN AMERICAN HISTORY

SPUTNIK/EXPLORER I
THE RACE TO CONQUER SPACE

MILESTONES
IN
AMERICAN HISTORY

THE TREATY OF PARIS

THE MONROE DOCTRINE

THE TRANSCONTINENTAL RAILROAD

THE ELECTRIC LIGHT

THE WRIGHT BROTHERS

THE STOCK MARKET CRASH OF 1929

SPUTNIK/EXPLORER I

THE CIVIL RIGHTS ACT OF 1964

SPUTNIK/ EXPLORER I

THE RACE TO CONQUER SPACE

SAMUEL WILLARD CROMPTON

CHELSEA HOUSE
PUBLISHERS
An imprint of Infobase Publishing

Cover: The Jupiter-C rocket, pictured here at the Army Ballistic Missile Agency in Huntsville, Alabama, launched America's first satellite, *Explorer I,* on January 31, 1958.

Sputnik/Explorer I: The Race to Conquer Space

Copyright © 2007 by Infobase Publishing

Chelsea House
An imprint of Infobase Publishing
132 West 31st Street
New York, NY 10001

ISBN-10: 0-7910-9357-3
ISBN-13: 978-0-7910-9357-3

Library of Congress Cataloging-in-Publication Data
Crompton, Samuel Willard.
  Sputnik/Explorer 1: the race to conquer space / Samuel Willard Crompton.
    p. cm. — (Milestones in american history)
  Includes bibliographical references and index.
  ISBN 0-7910-9357-3 (hardcover)
  1. Astronautics—Juvenile literature. I. Title. II. Series.

  TL793.C75 2007
  629.4—dc22   2006034127

Series design by Erik Lindstrom
Cover design by Ben Peterson

Printed in the United States of America

Bang NMSG 10 9 8 7 6 5 4 3 2 1

This book is printed on acid-free paper.

All links and Web addresses were checked and verified to be correct at the time of publication. Because of the dynamic nature of the Web, some addresses and links may have changed since publication and may no longer be valid.

CONTENTS

1   *Sputnik*   1

2   Science Fiction, Science Fact   13

3   *Explorer* and NASA   23

4   From Mercury to Gemini   35

5   Walking in Space   44

6   Setbacks   54

7   Saved by Saint Nick   63

8   One Giant Leap   74

9   Space in the Imagination   85

Chronology   93

Timeline   94

Notes   96

Bibliography   98

Further Reading   100

Index   102

Sputnik

Friday, October 4, 1957, dawned like most days of that decade. Millions of Americans rose with the sun, ate breakfast at home—there were few fast-food restaurants in 1957—and hastened off to the farm, factory, or office. The number of Americans who actually farmed for a living had dropped over the last few decades, while the number who toiled in factories or offices had increased.

Americans went to work by bus, subway, train, and automobile. Very few actually walked to work, as so many of their parents had done just a generation ago. Although only 20 years had passed since the Great Depression of the 1930s, American life had become unrecognizable in many ways. Americans ate more and better food, traveled more quickly and easily, and generally lived more comfortable lives than their parents.

On the morning of October 4, 1957, *Sputnik I* became the first artificial satellite to orbit the earth. The Soviet satellite was approximately the size of a basketball and weighed just 184 pounds (83.6 kilograms).

As they commuted to work and back, most Americans were preoccupied with local news, local stories, and the events of their normal, everyday lives. As they headed home that afternoon, they probably thought about work, family, and church, which were generally recognized as the pillars of American society. Some may have thought about a football or soccer game (perhaps with their children involved). Some may even have speculated about what might be on the television that evening; as it turned out, a new situation comedy, *Leave it to Beaver*, debuted that very night. If they read the *New York Times* (millions did), they might have been concerned about the flu epidemic that had affected 200,000 people in New York City alone. But it is likely that few Americans thought about space, satellites, or a "Race for Space," all of which would become household words in the weeks and months to come.

THE INTERNATIONAL GEOPHYSICAL YEAR

In 1950, an American scientist, Lloyd Berkner, had proposed that the 18 months between July 1957 and December 1958 be recognized as the International Geophysical Year (IGY), a time for scientists around the world to study matters having to do with the earth and its place in the universe. Agreements were reached, and nearly 70 nations participated in the IGY, with scientists meeting in many locations throughout the world. Eleven specific topics were approved for study, with satellite technology listed as one of the areas of interest. The IGY began in the summer of 1957 with little fanfare, but scientists were thrilled with some of the early progress being made. They were also taken aback to learn that both the Union of Soviet Socialist Republics (USSR) and the United States intended to send satellites into orbit at some point during the 18-month Geophysical Year.

THE SOVIETS ARE FIRST

The Soviet Union successfully sent an unmanned craft into space first. Sometime on the morning of October 4 (Moscow time), the USSR launched an immense rocket that fired a satellite into orbit. Named *Sputnik* (which translated to "fellow traveler"), the 184-pound satellite traveled at 18,000 miles per hour, orbiting the earth every 90 minutes or so. *Sputnik* made a rather annoying "beep . . . beep . . . beep" sound, which many

Americans claimed to hear on October 5 and for weeks afterward. Faint streaks were also observable in the morning and evening sky, though some of the reports of direct sightings were probably made by people seeking attention.

The *New York Times* pointed out that *Sputnik* was eight times heavier than the device the U.S. government hoped to place in orbit. Americans became edgy and downright apprehensive about their future. One of the core beliefs that drove American society was the idea that U.S. scientists and engineers were the world's best—and here the Russians were, outperforming them. The *Times* reported that Dr. Joseph Kaplan, who was chairman of the U.S. section of the International Geophysical Year, called the Russian achievement "fantastic."

However, concerned voices intruded on the admiration for the Russian accomplishment. In an open letter to the *New York Herald Tribune*, economist Bernard Baruch wrote about "The Lessons of Defeat":

> While we devote our industrial and technological power to producing new model automobiles and more gadgets, the Soviet Union is conquering space. While America grumbles over taxes and cuts the cloak of its defense to the cloth of its budget, Russia is launching intercontinental missiles. Suddenly, rudely, we are awakened to the fact that the Russians have outdistanced us in a race which we thought we were winning. It is Russia, not the United States, who has had the imagination to hitch its wagon to the stars and the skill to reach for the moon and all but grasp it. America is worried. It should be.[1]

Just as Americans started to get used to the incessant "beep . . . beep . . . beep," and just as they were getting accustomed to the idea that the Russians had beaten them to the punch, they were surprised again. Americans learned that *Sputnik II,* launched on November 3, 1957, weighed more than a thousand pounds, and actually carried a dog (named Laika, for its breed) to test how living beings would react to the challenge of weightlessness. American indignation continued to grow.

IKE AND NIKITA

In the autumn of 1957, Russian leaders could proudly boast that they had gotten the best of the United States. Until that very year, there had been several different men running the Kremlin in a collective dictatorship, but that changed in the summer of 1957, when Nikita Khrushchev emerged as the new strongman and sole leader of the USSR. As such, he was naturally compared with his American counterpart, Dwight Eisenhower.

There actually *were* some similarities between the two men. Both had been born in the 1890s; both had grown up in farming communities; and both outwardly displayed mannerisms that made them seem "down home," belying their actual intelligence and sophistication. But underneath these similarities, there was a big difference: "Ike" (as Americans called him) was a capitalist, a believer in free enterprise, and "Nikita" (as many people called him) believed in Russian socialism, which had grown out of the ideas of Karl Marx and Vladimir Lenin.

In the days and weeks following the orbit of *Sputnik I*, Khrushchev reveled in the newfound publicity and attention he received from the rest of the world. Frequently given to exaggeration, he claimed that this was just the beginning; that the USSR would soon launch bigger and better satellites and that it would leave the United States behind in the dust. For his part, Eisenhower kept a low profile, trying to act as if the news of *Sputnik* did not bother him. An old hand at public relations, Eisenhower did manage to calm the nerve of the American public, but his aides and friends knew better—Ike was furious over the Russians getting into space ahead of the United States.

After the Russians launched *Sputnik II* and the dog Laika, Eisenhower felt compelled to ease American concerns. He made a television address from Oklahoma City on November 7, just four days after the second *Sputnik* was launched into

On November 3, 1957, Laika became the first animal to orbit the earth. The Russian dog was found on the streets of Moscow and beat out two other dogs for the right to travel to space.

space. Mentioning that the Soviets were celebrating the fortieth anniversary of the 1917 revolution that brought them to power, Eisenhower said:

> We know of their rigorous educational system and their technological achievements. But we see all this happening under a political philosophy that postpones again and again the promise to each man that he will be allowed to be himself and to enjoy according to his own desires the fruit of his own labor. We have long had evidence—recently, very dramatic evidence—that even under such a system it is possible to produce some

remarkable material achievements. When such competence in things material is at the service of leaders who have so little regard for things human, and who command the power of an empire, there is danger ahead for free men everywhere.[2]

Eisenhower was just warming up. He admitted the importance of the Russian achievement, but hinted at greater American accomplishments to come. He spoke of the importance of keeping American alliances with other parts of the free world strong and indicated that taxes would have to be raised in order to keep American defenses in tip-top shape. But Eisenhower saved the most important part of his speech for the end, when he called for a renewed American effort in the areas of science, technology, and higher education:

> We should, among other things, have a system of nationwide testing of high school students; a system of incentives for high-aptitude students to pursue scientific or professional studies; a program to stimulate good-quality teaching of mathematics and science; provision of more laboratory facilities, and measures, including fellowships, to increase the output of qualified teachers. . . . We need scientists. In the ten years ahead they say we need them by thousands more than we are now presently planning to have.[3]

The president had spoken. High schools, colleges, and universities saw the handwriting on the wall. If they wanted financial assistance from the federal government, they would have to produce more scientists and engineers, and, one might suspect, fewer sociologists and philosophers.

PROJECT VANGUARD

Even though President Eisenhower wanted more scientists, everyone knew it would take years for young people to be trained and to become proficient in this discipline. For the moment, the United States had to rely upon the men (and women) who had taken its scientific departments to their current state of performance. Luckily there was not one, but two departments hard at work on developing satellite technology.

The U.S. Navy and the National Science Foundation had been working on their satellite program, appropriately named Vanguard. The U.S. Army had been working with the Jet Propulsion Laboratory to develop its satellite, named *Explorer*. Both programs were close to being ready, but neither had been able to test its missile systems to the fine degree one would have hoped. Given the choice between the two, Eisenhower gave the first try to Vanguard because of its connection to the National Science Foundation. (He was anxious for the U.S. space program to be affiliated with a science organization rather than a military one.) Everyone who was in the know turned their eyes to Cape Canaveral, Florida, which would be the launch site for this, and virtually all American space initiatives that followed.

CAPE CANAVERAL

Just a decade earlier, Cape Canaveral had been one of the least attractive or desirable sections of the Florida coast. Named by Spanish explorers in the 1540s, Cape Canaveral (which means "canebreak" in Spanish) had long been known as a treacherous spot for mariners, and in the century since Florida had entered the Union, its population had not grown by any significant degree. Insects abounded on the Cape, and those who came to Florida looking for fun in the sun avoided this area. But the same circumstances—isolation—that made the Cape undesirable for tourists made it nearly perfect for the budding U.S. space program: Here, one could work in privacy. There was the added benefit that any failed missile launch, or explosion of dangerous gases would probably occur over the open waters of the Atlantic Ocean, not in an urban or suburban area.

The U.S. Navy/Vanguard team had to move with great speed, because the American public was eager to see their country keep up with the Soviet Union. The rocketry equipment arrived at the Cape by early November and the tiny, three-pound satellite was in place days later. But there were numerous delays, both because of the need to check and recheck the missile system and because of the weather, which could shift very rapidly (Cape Canaveral lies close to the Atlantic Gulf Stream). A veteran journalist, who had covered the budding space program from the start, later described what it was like for him and his fellow reporters:

> In the nose of the seventy-two-foot rocket was a tiny pretender to the sacrosanctum of space, a 3.2 pound shot-put 6.4 inches in diameter. The secrecy wraps were suddenly thrown aside. For four hours J. Paul Walsh, deputy director of the project, and Herschel Schooley of the Department of Defense gave a detailed briefing to over a hundred newsmen.[4]

The newsmen were present for the briefing but they learned they could not be inside the Cape Canaveral site during the launch itself. For the next several days, the journalists huddled on a sand dune just south of the Cape, where they could see the red and yellow lights of *Vanguard TV3* blinking in the distance. If a countdown commenced, they would learn of it soon enough:

> Driftwood was precious and we collected all of it we could for firewood. During the long nights newsmen huddled around the fires, eating sandwiches, drinking beer and coffee. Sometimes we sang songs but our eyes never wandered far from the candy-striped Vanguard gantry [holding crane] which glowed like a jeweled skyscraper just across the harbor.[5]

It seems ironic that journalists about to witness the start of the American space age had to rely on burning driftwood for warmth, but life in the 1950s abounded in such ironies. Americans were the most technologically advanced people in the world—with radios, automobiles, and televisions—but many middle-aged citizens could remember a time of primitive outhouses rather than toilets and wood stoves rather than oil-fueled boilers. The countdown started early in the morning of December 6, 1957.

Hours went by, during which the engineers and scientists checked and rechecked every instrument. Despite their knowledge and proficiency, these men (there were no women in the group) had never launched this missile before. There could be all sorts of problems, and the early-stage computers the technicians used were primitive compared to the ones that high school students use today.

> At 11:44 AM, the rocket's umbilical cords dropped away and bounced off the catch net. Thirty seconds later a spurt of flame appeared at the base. For two seconds everything appeared normal. The rocket actually began to rise. Suddenly a tongue of orange flame darted out of the base, briefly climbed the west side of Vanguard, then fanned out toward the ocean side of the rocket and blossomed immediately into a massive, roiling ball of red fire and black smoke.[6]

Ten seconds of fire and flame were all it took before *Vanguard TV3* collapsed. The lower stages of the rocket were melted; some of the upper stage remained; and, somehow, the little three-pound satellite miraculously survived. It lay on the ground, blinking and beeping, a sign of American technological failure.

MAN OF THE YEAR

Americans were stunned and dismayed. Once more, their scientists and engineers had come off second best to the Russians.

The editors of *Time* were patriotic Americans. They would have loved to put an American rocket scientist on the cover

The U.S. Navy's Vanguard Project was created in 1955 to compete with the Soviet Union's Sputnik program. After a failed launch attempt on December 6, 1957, the second rocket, *Vanguard I,* successfully traveled to space on March 17, 1958.

of their magazine, naming him "Man of the Year." But when they analyzed the situation, and looked at the events of October through December 1957, they reluctantly came to the conclusion that one man—and one man only—could be "Man of the Year": It had be to Nikita Khrushchev.

The Russian leader appeared on the cover of *Time* in January 1958. The composite illustration made him look both confident and superior. On his head, he wore a crown composed of the palaces of the Russian Kremlin; in his hands, he held a set of antennae and wires that were made to resemble *Sputnik*. Khrushchev had never looked so good. The Soviet system had never seemed so triumphant. But the race for space (the expression started to enter American parlance that year) was only beginning.

Science Fiction, Science Fact

One has to travel back 90 years before the launch of *Sputnik* to find a literary reference that speaks to the heart of the matter. One has to turn to the work of French novelist Jules Verne.

Born in 1828, Verne reached the high point of his career in the 1860s. In 1865, he published *From the Earth to the Moon*, which was translated into English a year or two later. Verne began with the following hypothesis: that Americans were the world's natural engineers, just as Italians were the best musicians, and Germans the best logicians.

THE GUN CLUB OF BALTIMORE

Verne's novel begins at a gun club, located in Baltimore, Maryland, whose members were quite downcast with the end of the American Civil War in 1865. They had enjoyed great success

French author Jules Verne was a pioneer in the genre of science fiction and wrote one of the first novels about space travel when he published *From the Earth to the Moon* in 1865. Amazingly, there are many similar elements in Verne's novel to NASA's Apollo missions, including the name of the command modules: *Columbiad* and *Columbia*.

in the making and casting of cannon, but suddenly they were unemployed. (Verne pointed out that most of the Gun Club associates lacked an arm or a leg, an occupational hazard for men of that profession.) So distressed were they that the Gun Club associates were delighted when their president, a man named Impey Barbicane, announced he had a novel project that would occupy them for years to come. Rather than go straight to the subject, he worked his way around it, saying that the Gun Club members needed an outlet for their tremendous inventive energies. Finally, he came to the point: He wanted the Gun Club to build a cannon large enough to fire a spaceship to the moon.

Of course, he did not use the word *spaceship*, and the craft he described was more Victorian than twentieth century, but Impey Barbicane was speaking the language of future space inventors, just the same. When members of the Gun Club badgered him about the what, how, why, and where of the topic, he referred them to a letter sent by the Harvard College Observatory, which answered most of their questions, at least those connected with the moon.

Barbicane had questioned the Harvard Observatory on a number of matters. His questions included:

1. Is it possible to transmit a projectile up to the moon?
2. What is the exact distance which separates the earth from its satellite? . . .
5. What point in the heavens ought the cannon to be aimed at which is intended to Discharge the projectile?
6. What place will the moon occupy in the heavens at the moment of the projectile's departure?[7]

The answers were as follows:
Yes was the answer to question one.

The moon is 252,000 miles (405,500 kilometers) at its farthest distance from Earth, and 225,700 miles (363,000 kilometers) at its closest. Naturally, it was preferable to fire the projectile at a time when the moon was closer.

Concerning question number five, the answer was that the cannon should be pointed to the zenith of the horizon, and this required that it be fired from a location somewhere between zero and 28 degrees north latitude or zero and 28 degrees south latitude. At that time, long before Hawaii had become part of the United States, the southernmost areas of the nation were in southern Florida and southern Texas. This led to an immediate scrap between the two states, both of which demanded the honor of being the blast-off point for the spaceship built by the Baltimore Gun Club.

Lobbied by both Texas and Florida, Impey Barbicane and his committee decided upon the latter, which made the Texans furious. Not long after the decision was made, Barbicane and leading members of the Gun Club descended on Florida's west coast, at Tampa, headed inland about 12 miles, and found a place called Stone's Mill. It was there that they decided they would launch the projectile, which they called *Columbiad*.

The details of the projectile and cannon's manufacture were lengthy, but they are not important for our modern-day understanding of what was about to transpire. What was remarkable—and still is today—is that Verne described a countdown and blast-off situation that very closely resembled what would later happen in Florida, only on the *east coast*, at Cape Canaveral, about 90 years later:

Thirty-five!—thirty-six!—thirty-seven!—thirty-eight!—thirty-nine!—forty! FIRE!!!

Instantly Murchison pressed with his finger the key of the electric battery, restored the current of the fluid, and discharged the spark into the breech of the Columbiad. An appalling, unearthly report followed instantly, such as can be compared to nothing whatever known, not even to the roar of thunder, or the blast of volcanic explosions! No words can convey the slightest idea of the terrific sound! An immense spout of fire shot up from the bowels of the earth as from a crater. The earth heaved up, and with great difficulty some few spectators obtained a momentary glimpse of the projectile victoriously cleaving the air in the midst of the fiery vapors![8]

Reading and rereading Jules Verne, one sometimes has to pause and remember that he wrote these words in 1865, not 1965. He was a man ahead of his time.

THOSE WHO FOLLOWED VERNE

Jules Verne's work was amazingly popular in France, England, the United States, and elsewhere. Although first published in 1865, the major effects of *From the Earth to the Moon* came about 30 years later, when a new generation read the Frenchman's novel. One of the first of this generation to act on Jules Verne's vision was the English author H. G. Wells. Wells's novel *War of the Worlds* was first published in England in 1898. Thousands upon thousands of readers were both thrilled and appalled by the vision he presented.

Until that time, most discussions of science and outer space had made humans the actors, and the stars and planets the backdrop. H. G. Wells turned this around in his scary description of Martian plans to conquer the earth. These Martians were more scientifically developed than humans, but the aliens' own physical strength and life force had been sapped by their science and technology. The Martians foresaw the end of their own planet, and came to Earth seeking a place to conquer and turn into their own.

To make a long story short, the Martians arrived, landing in southern England. They were horrible, grotesque to behold, and their technology far in advance of humans. The Martians seemed poised to wipe out the British, and perhaps the rest of the world, but they succumbed to a disease for which they had no immunity.

SCIENCE FICTION TURNS TO FACT

In Verne's and Wells's time, many people of western Europe and the United States had ideas of rockets, boosters, and capsules that were only that—ideas. But even then, there were a handful of men around the world eagerly working on rockets that were meant for more practical purposes than to appear within the pages of science-fiction novels.

Leading the way in the push toward space was a Russian named Konstantin Tsiolkovsky. Born in 1857, Tsiolkovsky was

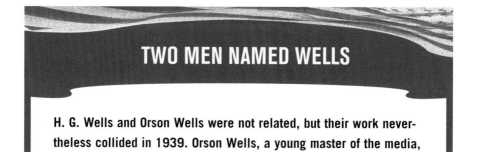

TWO MEN NAMED WELLS

H. G. Wells and Orson Wells were not related, but their work nevertheless collided in 1939. Orson Wells, a young master of the media, decided to put on a major radio show of *War of the Worlds*.

Born in Wisconsin in 1915, Orson Wells was only 23 when he put his show on the radio. Working with the celebrated actor John Houseman, Wells performed a dramatic rendition of *War of the Worlds* on October 30, 1938. Although meant as a Hollywood stunt, it caused panic throughout the Northeast region of the United States, where the show aired. Hundreds of thousands of Americans panicked. As they listened to the frightening descriptions of Martians landing in spacecrafts, Americans thought it was really happening. Many fled. New York City experienced serious panic for the next day, and it was a good 48 hours before life returned entirely to normal. Americans had had their first major brush with outer space, and it had taken place over the airwaves of their living-room radios.

attracted to science from a young age; he was influenced early on by the work of Jules Verne. By the time he became a school-teacher at the age of 21, he was devoting all his spare time to the study of rockets. Tsiolkovsky and those who followed him applied English scientist Sir Isaac Newton's third law of motion to the study of rockets and science: For every action, there is an equal and opposite reaction.

This law means that the power created by the gas and fumes of a rocket would move backward and that the rocket would move forward with equal force. How Tsiolkovsky managed to test his theories without any government funding or time off from work is one of the mysteries of rocket science. He worked out the theory and principle of the multistage rocket by 1903. This meant that parts of a rocket would drop away as their fuel was spent, giving even greater force to the other rocket parts as they left Earth's gravity field.

Despite making great strides in his research, Tsiolkovsky received almost no attention from the government of Russia, and only received some honor and money later in life, in the 1930s. The Communist government of the Soviet Union was not particularly interested in the conquest of space; they wanted to use rockets in war.

This brings us to Tsiolovosky's American counterpart. Born in Massachusetts in 1882, Robert Goddard was a sickly youth. His mother died of tuberculosis—a very common disease at the time—and his own lungs were stricken with the disease, but he survived. Due to his fragile health, Goddard often studied at home rather than in the public schools, and in the fall of 1899, at the age of 17, he made the breakthrough that would sustain his entire lifework.

It was October 19. Goddard had recently read H. G. Wells's *War of the Worlds*. He later described his breakthrough:

> On this day I climbed a tall cherry tree at the back of the barn ... and as I looked toward the fields at the east, I

imagined how wonderful it would be to make some device
that had even the possibility of ascending to Mars, and how
it would look upon a small scale, if sent up from the meadow
at my feet. . . . It seemed to me then that a weight whirling
around a horizontal shaft, moving more rapidly above than
below, could furnish lift by virtue of the greater centrifugal
force at the top of the path.[9]

Many years passed before Goddard used the idea he got
from watching *War of the Worlds*. He regained his health and
studied physics at Clark University, near his home. He earned
his Ph.D. and began teaching at Clark, but his attention was
focused more than ever on rockets. He married in 1923 and
seemed to be living the life of a conventional academic.

In 1919, he wrote an article for *Smithsonian* magazine, specu-
lating about the possibility of space flight. The article won more
attention than scientific articles usually do, but almost all of it
negative. The *New York Times* and other media mocked Goddard's
ideas. Faced with this discouragement and ridicule, Goddard
withdrew into himself. He, his wife, and a couple of close friends
were therefore the only ones to work on his rocket experiments in
the 1920s. His neighbors thought he was eccentric; his fellow pro-
fessors regarded him with detached amusement; and the scientific
community knew little to nothing about what he did.

And there it might have remained if not for Charles
Lindbergh.

Lindbergh was the first man to fly nonstop from New York
to Paris alone, a feat he performed in 1927. Just two years later,
he came to Worcester, Massachusetts, and spent a lot of time
with Goddard. Unlike many others, Lindbergh believed in the
possibility of rockets and space flight almost from the start.

Perhaps it was the admiration of one aviator for another.
Perhaps it was because Lindbergh was, like Goddard, a very
private man who had his own troubles with bad publicity. For

Robert Goddard, pictured here in 1938 at Roswell, New Mexico, developed several rockets for the U.S. government between 1932 and 1945. Goddard's first liquid-fueled rocket was launched on March 16, 1926, in Auburn, Massachusetts, but traveled just 41 feet during a 2.5-second flight.

whatever reason, Lindbergh became Goddard's greatest supporter. He introduced Goddard to the wealthy Guggenheim family, who provided money for new rocket tests. By that time, Goddard had had enough of Massachusetts and his neighbors. Using the money provided by the Guggenheims, he moved to the desert area of New Mexico to conduct tests.

Goddard never overcame his dislike of the press. He continued to distrust fellow scientists, and some of his inventions therefore did not reach the greater scientific community. But his personal success cannot be questioned. Between 1932 and 1945, Goddard designed, built, and fired off a large number of rockets in the New Mexico desert. Some were spectacular failures; others were merely dismal ones. But there were successes, too, and by the time of his death in August 1945, Goddard was fortunate to see that rocketry had moved from a fun idea to a genuine science. Science fiction (inspired by Jules Verne and H. G. Wells) had become science fact in the hands of men like Tsiolkovsky and Goddard.

Explorer and
NASA

By an interesting coincidence, Charles Wilson, the U.S. secretary of defense, was at the Army Ballistic Missile Agency in Alabama on the afternoon of October 4, 1957, when *Sputnik I* was launched. Apart from being surprised by the magnitude of the Russian accomplishment, Wilson wanted to know how soon the Army/Jet Propulsion Laboratory could move to launch a satellite of its own. The ever-optimistic Wernher von Braun replied that they could do it in 60 days, while the more cautious administrative chief said it would take up to 90. In either case, this was faster than what Wilson or the Eisenhower administration had expected.

THE GERMAN ELEMENT
The U.S. Army had been in the rocket "business" since 1945, when it took about 100 high-level German prisoners into

At the end of World War II, German engineer Wernher von Braun was cap-tured by the U.S. Army and brought to the United States. Von Braun had been one of the leading scientists in the development of Germany's V-2 Rocket program and played a similar role in shaping the United States' missile program. Pictured here is a V-2 rocket being launched at White Sands Proving Grounds in Las Cruces, New Mexico, in May 1946.

custody after World War II. Those Germans, who had worked on Hitler's V-2 Rocket program, were delighted to surrender to the Americans rather than the Russians; for their part, the Americans were pleased to take so many high-level engineers back to the United States.

The German prisoners spent some time on an island in Boston Harbor before being taken to White Sands, New Mexico, to form the core of a new United States missile program. The

30-year-old Wernher von Braun, the son of a Prussian aristo-crat, became their leader, and the Germans soon graduated from prisoner status to willing participants in the American program. In 1949, they were moved yet again, this time from White Sands to Alabama. By then, they had developed the beginnings of an American missile program. By 1957, when the news about *Sputnik* emerged, the Germans had nearly all become naturalized U.S. citizens, and they were pleased to be part of the effort to match the Russians in space.

When *Vanguard TV3* crashed to the ground on December 6, 1957, it was the U.S. Army's turn to attempt to launch a satellite into space.

THE BUILDUP

January 1958 turned out to be the coldest winter month experienced in Florida in many years. The U.S. Army team working on *Explorer,* and the U.S. Navy team, which had not given up on *Vanguard,* both struggled with ice and light snow, as well as the usual technical challenges.

Vanguard still had some opportunities. There were at least three countdowns in January 1958, each one ending in a "scrubbed" mission. By the end of January, attention shifted to the *Explorer* team, which had its Redstone Rocket ("Redstone" for the clay soil of Alabama) on a launchpad. A small three-pound satellite was in the upper cone of the missile. *Time* described the moment:

> A bright waxing moon rode through the racing cumu-lus clouds above Florida's Cape Canaveral. At the floodlit launching pad, a gangling service structure, standing like a jeweled skyscraper nestled against the U.S. Army's Jupiter-C rocket. A homely creature it was, its streamlined shell topped with a bucketlike piece and a long thin, cylindrical nose. This was the Explorer, the Promethean gift that the U.S. planned to fling against the invisible doors of space.[10]

The Redstone Rocket was the work of the U.S. Army, but the small satellite was produced by a handful of civilian scientists, most notably James Van Allen, a physicist from the University of Iowa. The rocket that would transport *Explorer I* began to heat up on the morning of January 31, 1958, and at the appointed time it blasted off without a hitch. "Never wavering on its course, the rocket rose faster and faster, cut through a layer of overcast and reappeared as a steadily diminishing spark burning its way out of sight."[11]

American observers at stations throughout the world were able to witness its progress. The first stage after blastoff lifted the missile 60 miles in the first 150 seconds. There followed a coasting flight of about 240 seconds, then the dramatic second stage, which lifted the rocket up to 200 miles above the earth (by now the nose had fallen off). The third- and fourth-stage intervals took the rocket to twice that height and put the tiny satellite into orbit at 18,000 miles per hour. Even the army scientists were slightly stunned by their own success.

IN THE SKIES

Explorer I soon reached the same level (600 miles high) previously attained by *Sputnik I* and *II*. Although *Explorer I* was much smaller and lighter than the Russian satellites (there was no thought of being able to lift a dog, or any other living being into space), it was also more sophisticated, sending back more reliable information than its Soviet counterparts. Within just a few days, American scientists were marveling over a trove of data and puzzling over some aspects of it as well.

In a short time, army scientists learned that the Geiger counter sent up with *Explorer I* to measure the level of radiation in the atmosphere was malfunctioning. No one knew why it was not working, but Van Allen (who had spent many years studying solar radiation) suspected it was because the Geiger counter could not handle the level of radiation coming its way. This was confirmed when *Explorer II* went up a month later and experienced the same difficulty. American scientists did not want to make a premature statement, so they waited until May 1, 1958, to go public with their findings, which were

☆ At 600 miles above the earth, radiation levels were more than 150 times higher than acceptable levels for humans.

☆ There were a series of belts in the radiation sphere that helped to protect the earth's atmosphere from solar radiation.

☆ The Geiger counters had stopped working because they were simply overloaded.

All of this could have been seen in a negative light, but the scientists assured the public that radiation shields could be designed so astronauts (the word had just entered the English language) would be able to venture into space.

CREATION OF NASA

Until 1958, there was no single U.S. space program; instead, there were the competing army and navy missile programs. But pressure began to build for a unified space program, with both a civilian and military aspect. President Eisenhower indicated his approval, and late in July 1958, he signed Public Law 85-568, which created the National Aeronautics and Space Administration (NASA).

NASA started operations in October 1958 and almost at once announced its plans to select a small group of potential astronauts. The criteria were extensive. The candidates had to be

☆ College graduates, with degrees in the physical sciences

☆ Graduates of a test-pilot school

☆ Possess 1,500 hours of flying time

☆ Under the age of 40, and

On April 9, 1959, the Mercury Seven astronauts were introduced to the American press by NASA. Pictured here from left to right: M. Scott Carpenter, Leroy Gordon Cooper, John H. Glenn Jr., Virgil I. Grissom Jr., Walter M. Schirra Jr., Alan B. Shepard Jr., and Donald K. Slayton.

☆ Five-feet-eleven or less (this was important because of the size of the space capsules planned for the future).

THE MERCURY SEVEN

Malcolm Scott Carpenter, Leroy Gordon Cooper Jr., Virgil I. Grissom, Walter M. Schirra Jr., Donald K. Slayton, John H. Glenn Jr., and Alan B. Shepard Jr., were chosen as the first astronauts, and presented to the press on April 9, 1959. It has often been noted that all seven were white, of Anglo-Saxon descent, Protestant, and from small-to-mid-sized towns. Not a single one was the product of one of the big cities or of an elite private university.

If the selection was made today, eyebrows would be raised over the lack of diversity in the team, but Americans in 1959 were absolutely thrilled with their new astronauts. Every magazine from *Time* to *Newsweek* lavished praise on the men and their dedication; they had been selected from about 450 candidates, nearly all of them test pilots in the U.S. Air Force. A classic moment at the first press conference came when someone asked all seven astronauts whether they expected to go to outer space and return to tell the tale. All seven raised their right hands in affirmation, but two of them, John Glenn and Walter Schirra, raised both hands.

At about this time, NASA was in the early stages of designing what would become the American missile and rocket center. The center was, and still is, located at Cape Canaveral, Florida. The Mercury Seven were all in Florida in the spring of 1961. So was the mission control team, which would later be moved to Houston, Texas. But even as the Americans got into place and readied the team, the Russians took off first.

YURI GAGARIN

The Russians had their equivalent to the Mercury Seven. A team of cosmonauts had been selected and trained by Sergei Korolev, leader of the Soviet space program. Korolev was a brilliant and driven man. Inspired by the writings of Konstantin Tsiolkovsky and others, he had set his heart on space exploration at a young age. But Korolev battled many foes throughout his life. One was the Soviet government of Premier Joseph Stalin, which had sent him to the Gulag, the infamous Russian concentration camps, in the late 1930s. Korolev survived that terrible experience and was rehabilitated during the regime of Nikita Khrushchev.

One of the cosmonauts was Yuri Gagarin. Born in 1927, Gagarin celebrated his birthday in March 1961. His wife also gave birth to their second daughter, so it was a time of celebration all around. Then, in that same month, Gagarin was chosen to be the first cosmonaut (and the first human being) to attempt to orbit the earth. To "orbit" means something quite different from flying in a plane. No one ever did this until April 12, 1961.

Vostok I blasted off at nine in the morning, Moscow time. Gagarin had a speed-stick control, but he was instructed to let the automatic flight plan take precedence. As a result, he was able to focus on the excitement of being the first person in orbit. Even today, some controversy surrounds Gagarin's flight. Did he head south and pass over Africa, or did he go due east and over the Pacific Ocean? Although his exact flight path is not known, it is certain that he flew at about 180 miles above the earth, making this the highest flight to that point.

Russian citizens learned about Gagarin's flight from the government-controlled radio news, which alerted them at about 10:00 A.M. Moscow time. The Soviet space program had this big advantage over the Americans. If a flight went poorly, Soviet space program directors would not release any information to the public, and no one would know. By contrast, the Americans working at Cape Canaveral were surrounded by media.

Luckily for Gagarin and his team, nothing went wrong. By 11:00 A.M., he was back on Russian soil. Another long-standing controversy is whether or not he successfully landed *Vostok I* or parachuted to safety. The Russian government held out for many years before admitting in the 1980s that Gagarin did indeed parachute back to Earth.

After the flight, Nikita Khrushchev and Gagarin had a long-distance telephone conversation:

Khrushchev: How did you feel in flight? How did the first spaceflight proceed?

Gagarin: I felt well. The flight was most successful. All the instruments of the spaceship worked full faultlessly. During the flight I could see the Earth from that great height. I could see the seas, mountains, big cities, rivers, and forests.

Khrushchev: Then you felt well?

On April 12, 1961, Soviet cosmonaut Yuri Gagarin became the first human to travel into space and orbit the earth. Gagarin's trip aboard the *Vostok I* spacecraft lasted one hour and 29 minutes and reached a height of 187 miles (301 kilometers) above the earth.

Gagarin: That's right, Nikita Sergevich. I felt fine in the spaceship, quite at home. Thank you once again for your kind message of congratulations and for your good wishes on the successful flight.

Khrushchev: I'm glad to hear your voice and to greet you. I shall be happy to meet with you in Moscow. You and I, together with all our people, shall celebrate this great exploit in the conquest of space. Let the whole country see what our country is capable of, what our great people and our Soviet science can do.

Gagarin: Let all other countries catch up with us now![12]

ALAN SHEPARD

The American astronauts and technicians at mission control were dismayed that the Russians had gotten into space first. American technology was coming on slowly and surely, but there was no way that the Mercury Seven could immediately duplicate what Yuri Gagarin had achieved in space. Therefore, they decided to attempt something a bit less ambitious: to put the first American into orbit.

Each of the Mercury Seven astronauts wanted to be first in space. The choice was not theirs to make; there was a small group of people at NASA who made the final selection. It was secretly decided that Alan Shepard would be the person to go. Born in New Hampshire, Shepard was the son of a U.S. Army colonel. He had risen fast in the ranks of the U.S. Air Force himself and was seen as perhaps the most hard-charging of that very competitive group of seven astronauts. Shepard would take off from Cape Canaveral and perform a very short flight in space, but the other six astronauts would all still participate in one way or another.

The launch was scheduled for May 2, 1961, but bad weather intervened. The fourth of May was also considered, and then scrapped, because the NASA meteorologist predicted excellent conditions for May 5.

Alan Shepard blasted off aboard *Freedom VII* at 9:34 A.M. Eastern Standard Time. He later recalled the event:

I had some idea of the huge variety of color and land masses and cloud cover which I would see from 100 miles up there. But no one could be briefed well enough to be completely prepared for the astonishing view that I got. My exclamation back to Deke [Slayton] about the beautiful site was completely spontaneous. It was breathtaking. To the south I could see where the cloud cover stopped at about Fort Lauderdale, and that the weather was clear all the way down past the Florida Keys. To the north I could see up the coast of the Carolinas to where the clouds just obscured Cape Hatteras. Across Florida to the west I could spot Lake Okeechobee, Tampa Bay and even Pensacola. . . . It was really stunning.[13]

Shepard was up in space for about 15 minutes. He descended very quickly, and his capsule came down in the waters near Bimini and Andros Island in the Bahamas. Just seven minutes after he splashed down, sailors from the USS *Lake Champlain* hauled him aboard the ship. They cleaned him up and doused him in champagne. Even though Shepard's flight was very brief compared to Yuri Gagarin's, Americans rejoiced. President John F. Kennedy awarded a special medal to Shepard, and the scientists at NASA began to believe that they would catch up with the Russians soon.

THE ROAD TO VIENNA AND BERLIN

Americans were thrilled with Shepard's performance. President Kennedy was so pleased and impressed that he went before Congress on May 25, just three weeks after the flight, with a special message: He wanted America to go to the moon. It was an intense moment. Kennedy asked for $1.8 billion in additional funding that year, partly for defense, partly for international aid, but a sizeable chunk of it was for space exploration. He was serious about the goal, and wanted an American to land on the moon before the decade was over. Even as he made his speech, Kennedy knew that he would be traveling in a few days. He and Nikita Khrushchev had made plans to meet in Vienna, Austria, for their first "summit" conference; the tradition had been established by Khrushchev's visit to President Eisenhower in 1959.

Kennedy and his wife, Jacqueline, flew from Washington, D.C., to Paris first for their meetings with French president Charles de Gaulle. The French leader, like so many others, was greatly charmed by the First Lady, and for a time, President Kennedy called himself the man who had accompanied Jackie Kennedy to Paris. But then it was on to Vienna.

Kennedy and Khrushchev had very different personalities, as well as ideologies. The former was young, handsome, and vigorous, while the latter looked like a grandfather, and not always a very pleasant one at that.

Kennedy and Khrushchev met for several hours on June 3, 1961. No official transcript of the meeting was made, but Kennedy aides were certain that their man had been bullied and browbeaten. Word has it that Khrushchev threatened to go to war over Berlin, the former capital of Nazi Germany. The Americans, Russians, British, and French had occupied the city ever since the end of World War II, and the Russians had made efforts to kick their former war allies out. The issue had not escalated to war, but Khrushchev made some bold hints that he was now willing to go that far.

Kennedy was stunned by the older man's attack. The American president left believing, correctly, that Khrushchev was a dangerous man, and that the United States would have to resist his threats. Khrushchev left thinking, incorrectly, that Kennedy was an indecisive young man who could be bullied in the future. The meeting marked a renewal of cold war tensions.

From Mercury
to Gemini

The race for space continued. Toward the end of 1961 and at the beginning of 1962, mission control and the Mercury Seven prepared for a more ambitious project. The United States had been thrilled to put Alan Shepard in space, but he had only remained there about 15 minutes. Now there was a desire to have an astronaut orbit the earth, and to stay up in space for several hours.

Months of preparation went into this project. About 20,000 people at NASA were involved in one way or another. Everything had to be checked and rechecked a dozen times, if not more. NASA and the U.S. astronauts worked under a greater burden than their Russian counterparts. The American newspaper, radio, and television media all knew when a launch was approaching, and they were determined to have their questions answered. By contrast, the Russians could launch when they wanted, and, if things went wrong, no one ever knew (at least not for many years).

John Glenn was selected for the second mission. He stood out, even among such a group of dedicated and competitive men. Born in Cambridge, Ohio, in 1921, he had been a very young U.S. pilot in World War II, and then a more mature and seasoned one in Korea. In 1957, Glenn had broken a record by flying the first supersonic jet flight across the continental United States. That was the same year that the Russians launched *Sputnik*, and Glenn quickly saw that the center of action was transitioning from jet flight to space capsules. He competed for, and won, his place among the Mercury Seven. When selected for the program, Glenn was close to the cut-off age; he was also the heaviest of the astronauts, and had to lose a few pounds. None of this detracted from his ability and skill, however; he was always among the fittest of men.

THE FIRST AMERICAN ORBIT(S)

On February 20, 1962, Glenn was ready. He woke up at 1:30 A.M. and prepped for his takeoff, scheduled for five in the morning. At the time he awoke, Glenn learned that there was a chance he would not even fly that day because of the weather. But the skies cleared early that morning, and soon he was confident that the mission was a go.

Even today, with all the technology to which society is accustomed, there is something truly awesome about the power of rockets, boosters, and capsules. Glenn knew all about the hardware, but he had not yet experienced the thrill, and fear, that might accompany an actual blastoff. Climbing up into the capsule at seven in the morning, Glenn had to squeeze to get his frame inside *Friendship VII*. The capsule did not have any extra room; it was a tight fit for any man. As Glenn recounted:

> You are 74 feet above the ground, and the booster is so tall that it sways slightly in a heavy gust of wind. In fact, I could

On February 20, 1962, John Glenn became the first U.S. astronaut to orbit the earth when *Friendship VII* was launched from Cape Canaveral, Florida. The space capsule made three orbits around the earth over a period of four hours and 55 minutes.

set the whole structure to rocking a bit myself, just by moving back and forth in the couch.[14]

During these moments of waiting, Glenn was in constant radio contact with Shepard below. It must have been comforting for Glenn to know that Shepard was the only other American to have gone into outer space. Glenn recalled:

Blastoff came at 9:47 A.M. The rocket and capsule moved with great speed toward space. At 2 minutes and 11 seconds

after launch we jumped the third hurdle right on schedule
when the two big outboard booster engines shut down and
dropped away. We were out of the atmosphere by now, and
had built up enough speed so that all that we needed was
the long, final push from the sustainer engine to drive us
into orbit.[15]

As Glenn continued upward, he lost radio communication with Cape Canaveral, but mission control had known this
would happen. Soon he established contact with an American
team in Nigeria, the first of a number of groups set up around
the world, long in advance. Glenn later remembered the thrill
of seeing his first sunset from the space capsule. He was over
the Indian Ocean:

I saw a total of four sunsets before the day was over—three
during the flight and a final one after I landed and had been
picked up by the destroyer. Each time I saw it set, the sun
was slightly to my left, and I turned the spacecraft a little on
its yaw axis to get a better view. One thing that interested
me was the length of the twilight. The brilliant band of light
along the horizon was visible for up to five minutes after the
sun went down.[16]

Glenn was moving along like clockwork, but as he entered
his second orbit of the earth, the people at mission control
became anxious. There was a button flashing, indicating that
something was wrong with the packs that centered the heat
shield on *Friendship VII*. All pilots, technicians, and scientists
knew that Glenn and his craft would be exposed to a tremendous amount of heat as he reentered Earth's atmosphere at
the end of his flight. Some estimates ran as high as 3,000°F
(1,649°C), making this the scariest part of the entire mission. If
the heat shield was ajar, or just off by a few inches, that could
make all the difference, leaving Glenn to burn to death.

The first comments mission control made were measured, asking Glenn if he saw any lights flashing or signals that something was wrong. Naturally, these questions threw Glenn off, and he asked what mission control meant. For a time, he was given no clear answer.

Before long, Glenn was in his third orbit. As he approached the West Coast of the United States, he spoke with Shepard, whose job it was to guide him down. By now, Glenn had been alerted to the danger, but both he and mission control believed that the flashing light was probably an error. They took the chance. They had to, because Glenn could not stay up in space indefinitely. He landed in the Pacific Ocean, without any major problems. The heat shield held throughout the tremendous fire burn of reentry into the earth's atmosphere.

Perhaps no American pioneer ever returned to a louder and more sincere welcome. Glenn received a medal from President Kennedy and spoke before a joint session of the two houses of Congress. And, days later, he had a parade up Broadway in Lower Manhattan. Glenn received tremendous honors and he took them all in stride. He showed a combination of humility and self-assuredness that made him the man of the hour, if not the entire year.

THE GEMINI NINE

The Mercury missions had gone well, but it was time to move on. NASA announced its new selection of astronauts in October 1962. Nine new men were added to the astronaut roster; the most prominent of which was Neil Armstrong, who would become famous in the future.

NASA specifically declared its intention to have more engineers in this second astronaut group. The first group—the Mercury Seven—had largely been chosen for their skill and experience as test pilots; the nine men of the second group were mainly engineers. Even so, they continued to be white, middle-class, Protestant Americans, mostly from small towns.

Neil Armstrong, Frank Borman, Charles Conrad Jr., James Lovell Jr., James A. McDivitt, Elliott M. See Jr., Thomas P. Stafford, Edward H. White II, and John W. Young were a fascinating group. They were not as close as the Mercury Seven had been, partly because they were not solely test pilots. The Gemini Nine, or the New Nine, as they were called, collectively were more educated than the Mercury Seven, with a smattering of master's degrees in complex, technical topics. Only three and a half years had passed since the selection of the Mercury Seven; but the new group proved that NASA wanted its star performers to be distinguished in academic circles, as well as flying ones.

Just weeks after the new astronauts were introduced to the press, the United States experienced one of the greatest crises of the entire cold war. In mid-October, President Kennedy learned that Russian missiles placed in Communist Cuba would be able to target American cities on the East Coast. Kennedy called in his advisors for a quick and intense briefing at the White House. There were those who favored ignoring the matter for the moment, those who called for a measured response, and others who wanted an all-out strike on those Russian missiles in Cuba. The fact that the United States had missiles of its own in Turkey, pointed at the Soviet Union, hardly seemed to enter the equation.

Advised by his younger brother Robert Kennedy, who was now attorney general of the United States, President Kennedy decided on a measured response. He went on television to tell the American people of the danger, and he announced a quarantine of the naval space around Cuba, but he did not take immediate action. For several days, Russian ships continued to steam toward Cuba, suggesting that a confrontation in those waters could bring about World War III.

The scientists and engineers of the U.S. space program played no part in the events of October 1962; they were observers, like almost everyone else. But there was a general perception that if the Russians had more advanced missiles and if they could use that fact to blackmail the United States, it would somehow be NASA's fault.

Fortunately, the situation did not come to that. Days after Kennedy's television address to the American people, Khrushchev had his ships turn around. The Cuban Missile Crisis

THE COSMODROME

It was top secret from the very beginning. The Russians did not want the United States or other countries to know the whereabouts of their astronauts or rockets. Located on a major river in what is now the country of Kazakhstan, the Cosmodrome was well hidden for several years. The general American public did not learn about it until decades later, but top-level American leaders learned about it through U.S. spy planes flying over Soviet air space.

There, in a remote and rather inhospitable part of the Soviet Union, Sergei Korolev trained his cosmonauts and planned his many launches and probes. The Soviet Union is much farther north than Cape Canaveral, so the Soviets had to deal with harsh weather. Due to its more northerly location, the Cosmodrome created greater difficulties for the Russians throughout the race for space. Even more challenging, though, was the lack of teamwork the Russians faced. The Americans had about 40,000 people involved, either working directly for NASA or in private industry. The Russian space program had far fewer people in general, and only one man at the top. Korolev was a driven genius, a man of tremendous talent, but he was essentially working alone.

Korolev pulled off many successes, but there were also some dismal failures concealed from the press and the world at large. Driven by the top Soviet leaders, and by his own relentless quest, Korolev fell into ill health. He died after a bungled operation in 1966. His death was a major loss for Russian science.

During the summer of 1963, Soviet cosmonaut Valentina Tereshkova became the first woman to travel into space. Aboard *Vostok VI,* she orbited the earth 48 times over a 71-hour period.

came and went, in the space of about two weeks. But no one forgot it.

THE FIRST WOMAN IN SPACE

In the summer of 1963, the Russians put the first woman in space. Khrushchev was intent on pulling off everything before the Americans could. In June 1963, Valentina Tereshkova was sent up from the Russian Cosmodrome aboard *Vostok VI.*

The three-day flight went well. Tereshkova returned to Earth to receive the congratulations of Khrushchev and her fellow cosmonauts. Only later was it learned that she knew little about the space program and had been selected because she embodied many of the ideal qualities of a Russian Communist woman.

Premier Khrushchev made the most of this propaganda victory. He boasted that the Russians appreciated women more than the capitalist West, and that more women would go up in space. Sadly, this did not prove true. The Russians soon returned to an entirely male cosmonaut corps.

Americans looked on all this with wonder and more than a bit of envy. Maybe the Russians really were that far ahead, they thought. Perhaps Soviet science did have some big advantage over the capitalist West. If any one person could have calmed the hysteria, it was Kennedy. By 1963, he had become more than a political leader; he seemed to speak for and represent the best aspects of the American people. Kennedy did make one rather astonishing offer to work with the Russians in a joint space program, but it was quickly refused.

Sadly, Kennedy would not be able to see how the space race turned out. On November 22, 1963, he was shot and killed as his motorcade passed through the streets of Dallas, Texas. Four American presidents—Abraham Lincoln, James Garfield, William McKinley, and Kennedy—have been assassinated, but the last of these deaths has received the most attention. Had television existed in 1865, it is possible that Lincoln's death would have equaled Kennedy's assassination in the attention it received, but history ruled otherwise. The world would never again be the same.

Walking
in Space

For many years to come, most Americans would poignantly remember three big moments from the 1960s. The first was the Cuban Missile Crisis. The second was President Kennedy's assassination. The third was a major event in the space race between the Soviet Union and the United States, to be discussed in Chapter 8.

After Kennedy's assassination, his vice president, Lyndon B. Johnson, immediately replaced him as president. Sworn in as the thirty-sixth president, Johnson declared his intention to continue Kennedy's policies in most respects. For anyone in NASA listening—and there were many who did—that meant the race for space was still on.

President Johnson was never as strong a supporter of the space program as Kennedy had been. Johnson was most keenly interested in social programs, which he collectively called the

"Great Society" programs. Tremendous progress was made there. Medicare, a medical plan for senior citizens, was created in 1965. Major voting rights legislation was passed as well. By 1966, President Johnson seemed well on his way toward creating the Great Society at home in America. But there were still plenty of people plugging away at the space program, too.

NASA has often been criticized for its high budgets and exorbitant costs. To combat such concerns, the organization has routinely presented its budgets to the public, and major NASA leaders like James Webb and Tom Paine (who were NASA directors between 1960 and 1970) had to regularly testify before Congress. Given all the criticism it received, NASA felt it had to have a "squeaky clean" image, and it succeeded in doing so throughout the 1960s.

In 1964, the U.S. space program still seemed to lag behind the Soviet program. What Americans did not know—and what they would not know until the end of the cold war—was that the Russians were running out of steam. The Russian space budget had always been smaller than the United States', and the emphasis on secrecy often affected the progress made by Russian scientists. Then again, the Russians never openly stated what their goals were.

As early as the summer of 1961, President Kennedy had committed the United States to the goal of placing a man on the moon. It would happen by the end of the decade, he declared. By contrast, Khrushchev was tight-lipped. Conferring with his number-one space man, Sergei Korolev, Khrushchev put forth a two-pronged plan. First, he would emphasize accomplishments like having the first woman in space and the first person to walk in space; only then would he give his full attention to sending someone to the moon.

What Khrushchev failed to see—and it was really a failure of the imagination—is that the goal of having a man on the moon could pull in more popular support and more enthusiastic participation than anything else. Anything less would provoke a lukewarm reaction. By going for broke—as the Americans did in the mid-1960s—it was possible to capture the imagination and support of millions of people. Still, the race was not over.

VOSHKOD

The Russians unveiled their new *Voshkod* in 1964. Aware that the Americans were winning the propaganda war, Khrushchev decided on a novel approach. The early Russian flights had all been in one-seater *Vostoks*, and the Americans were well on the way to developing their two-seater *Gemini* capsules. Therefore, Khrushchev ordered Korolev to develop a brand-new *three-seater* spacecraft.

But there simply was not enough time. Korolev explained this, at length, to Khrushchev, but he received the same response. It must be done.

Given a hopeless task, and knowing that the dangers for the cosmonauts would increase, Korolev did the only thing he could. His designers ripped out the ejection seat from the old *Vostok* spacecraft and renamed the capsule *Voshkod* (a long time would pass before Western observers knew they had been fooled). Even with the seat removed, space was too tight, so Korolev reluctantly agreed that his cosmonauts would fly without any bulky space suits. Such a decision would have brought anger and alarm from the public in the United States. But Russians did not know; their space program still kept its secrets.

Voshkod took off on October 11, 1964. The Russian press had a field day. They had three cosmonauts in space while the Americans—for the moment at least—were doing nothing. But just one day into its flight, *Voshkod* was recalled. The cosmonauts were furious, then perplexed. Everything was going well; why would they be brought down?

The answer was simple: Nikita Khrushchev's government had been removed from power.

A NEW RACE

Khrushchev had been top boss in the Soviet Union for just about a decade. He had accomplished a good deal, especially in the space program, but his followers also remembered the

RUSSIAN DESCENTS

The Russians had a much tougher task than the Americans when it came to descent. Unlike Cape Canaveral, which is located right on the Atlantic Ocean, the Russians took off from what is now Kazakhstan. Their cosmonauts had to come down somewhere within the Soviet Union.

There was controversy from the very start. The Russian newspapers claimed that Yuri Gagarin landed safely in *Vostok I* in 1961; only years later was it revealed that he had parachuted to safety. The three-man crew of *Voshkod II* had it even tougher. The three cosmonauts came crashing down among trees in western Siberia, and could not be rescued that night. The men lit fires and fended off attacks from wolves before Soviet helicopters rescued them the following day.

All in all, it is easy to see why the Russians came to favor unmanned space probes. By the late 1960s, the Russians had sent probes to different sides of the moon. In the summer of 1969, realizing that the Americans were about to attempt a lunar landing, the Russians sent up an unmanned craft that was intended to bring back samples of the moon's surface. The probe did not survive.

When one realizes the many obstacles the Russian scientists and astronauts were up against—lack of funding, no ocean-based launch sites, and intense pressure from the government—it becomes easy to see how the Russians failed. The better question might be: How in the world did they do as well as they did?

In 1964, Leonid Brezhnev helped oust Soviet premier Nikita Khrushchev and took control of the Soviet Union. Brezhnev, who is pictured here with Cuban leader Fidel Castro in 1965, was in charge of running the Soviet space program prior to becoming general secretary of the Communist Party.

humiliating retreat during the Cuban Missile Crisis. They ejected Khrushchev in 1964 and replaced him with a collective leadership that included Leonid Brezhnev, who would emerge as the new leader throughout the next few years.

Khrushchev had made his share of errors, but his downfall was a definite negative for the Soviet space program. None of the collective leaders who followed him had Khrushchev's ambition to be the first in space, and none were willing to commit as much money as he did. There were other issues to take care of, both at home and abroad.

While it is indisputable that the United States had been catching up with the Russians by that point, it is also indisputable that Khrushchev's fall from power harmed the Soviet space program. What followed was a brand-new race, with the Americans often taking the lead.

THE FIRST SPACE WALKS

Both American and Russian engineers were keen to have their astronauts "walk" in space. Of course, it would not be an actual walk, not as we on Earth know it. The American engineers were a bit slower than the Russians, but, as usual, they also gave the matter more thought.

Space walks were actually secondary to an even more important objective: *rendezvous*. Until 1965, no spaceship—Russian or American—had been able to rendezvous, or meet up with another in space. There were good reasons for this; the logistical problems were enormous.

When a spaceship orbits the earth, or the moon for that matter, it is spinning around the planet at about 17,500 miles per hour. If another spaceship, presumably from the same nation and space program, wants to rendezvous, it will naturally get behind the other one and try to "catch up" with it. But that is how things work on land, not in space.

To "catch" the other spaceship, the one following must actually reduce its speed. This means the second, or chasing ship, will drop into a lower level of orbit, and will eventually "catch" the other one by slowing down instead of speeding up. The first attempts at rendezvous failed because the pilots could not shake their "Earth" behavior.

The Russians were first to walk in space. In March 1965, Russian cosmonaut Alexei Leonov stepped from his spacecraft.

He stayed "outside" in space for about 10 minutes, and enjoyed his moment until he had to fight his way back to the spacecraft. Leonov barely managed to get back inside. Even so, the Russian press celebrated; its cosmonauts had performed another "first."

The Americans were very aware that they again finished second. Chris Kraft, overall flight director for NASA, had this to say:

> Five days before we were to launch *Gemini III,* the Russians pulled off another space first. I never doubted that they timed this mission to preempt us and to turn the world's attention back to their own space program. They had the advantage of knowing exactly what we were going to do, and when, simply by reading the newspapers. So in the propaganda race we were running, the Russians could always count on the element of surprise.[17]

But it was one thing to hold the world's attention; it was another to pull off a space walk to perfection. *Gemini IV* blasted off on June 3, 1965. Aboard were Ed White and Jim McDivitt, both members of the second astronaut group, the New Nine of 1962. Once they were in a settled and calm orbit of the earth (this had become almost routine by 1965), White and McDivitt depressurized the cabin of the spacecraft to zero pounds per square inch. Gently they eased open the cockpit door, and Ed White stepped out into space. *Time* magazine reported:

> He floated lazily on his back. He joked and laughed. He gazed down at the Earth, 103 miles below, spotted the Houston-Galveston Bay area where he lived and tried to take a picture of it. Like a gas station attendant, he checked the spacecraft's thrusters, wiped its windshield. Ordered to get back into the capsule, he protested like a scolded kid. "I'm doing great," he said. "It's fun. I'm not coming in."[18]

Even though White was on a microphone and could be heard at mission control, no one, including himself, has ever been able to completely describe the amazing feeling of joy and liberation he experienced on this space walk. White stayed outside the cabin for 20 minutes, and it took more than polite urging to

KRAFT, KRANZ, AND HODGE

In 1965, as the United States set the record for time in space (four days), it became imperative to have mission control operate on a 24-hour basis, straight through the flight. This was accomplished by creating three teams of flight controllers, each one led by an experienced flight director.

Chris Kraft led the first eight-hour group, dubbed the Red Team. Kraft had been at mission control from the beginning and was considered the "father" of the brotherhood of flight controllers.

Gene Kranz had been hired by Kraft back in 1961. Still a young man, Kranz was known for a nearly fanatical approach to detail; he wanted to know everything that was happening or that could happen. During the *Gemini IV* mission, Kranz led the second eight-hour team, known as the White Team. His wife, Marta, knitted a handsome white sweater for the occasion, and Kranz wore it on the first day. To his surprise, his fellow flight controllers turned the TV camera on him for a minute to admire the new sweater. From that time on, it was standard that Marta would knit a new sweater for each important mission for which her husband was a flight director (this was shown in the 1995 film *Apollo 13*).

Finally, John Hodge directed the Blue Team. Between them, Kraft, Kranz, and Hodge kept in touch with the astronauts virtually every moment of their flight. This set a standard for mission control that has continued throughout the space program.

During NASA's *Gemini IV* mission in June 1965, Ed White became the first American to make a space walk. White is pictured here 103 miles above the earth during his 20-minute walk.

get him to return. Down on the ground, Kraft was upset by the lack of discipline showed at this key moment, but most people understood White's reluctance. By the summer of 1965, with White's space walk completed, the Americans were dead even with the Russians, and they were about to pull into the lead.

RENDEZVOUS

A Russian and an American had both walked in space. But until then, no one had pulled off a real rendezvous in space. The logistical problems were explained earlier. Once in orbit, a spacecraft must actually slow down, in order to catch another one. This took some thought and many trial simulations on the ground, but it was not done in space until December 1965, when *Gemini VI* rendezvoused with *Gemini VII*.

Neil Armstrong and Dave Scott attempted to do the second rendezvous in 1966. Armstrong and Scott blasted off an hour after the spaceship *Agena*, which they intended to catch. Through some impressive technical maneuvers, Armstrong and Scott caught up with and finally connected to, or docked with, the *Agena*. But the situation went downhill from there. Things at mission control had been going so well for so long that the flight directors must have been surprised and anxious when the word came down:

> We have serious problems here. We're . . . we're tumbling end over end up here. We're disengaged from the Agena.[19]

The flight directors immediately suspected something was wrong with the *Agena*—its computer, perhaps. But when attempts to reengage failed, mission control aborted the flight, telling Armstrong and Scott to make a quick splashdown in the Pacific Ocean. No one was harmed, and important lessons were learned. The problems that day had actually belonged to the spacecraft, rather than the *Agena*.

Armstrong later expressed his disappointment:

> I was very depressed at this point. We had not completed all the things we wanted to do. . . . We'd spent a lot of taxpayers' money, and they hadn't gotten their money's worth out of it.[20]

This disappointment did not last. Only three years later, Armstrong would fly an even more important mission, the one that made him one of the most famous astronauts.

Setbacks

Only now, many years after the fact, do we see the U.S. and Soviet space programs as they truly were. In the years when the events happened, and for some time afterward as well, Americans and Russians tended to think all was well with their "squeaky clean" space programs. This was not so. The Russians suffered more than the Americans, most especially because of the pressure put on the space program by their political leaders. Two men are prime examples of a system gone wrong.

SERGEI KOROLEV

By 1965, Sergei Korolev had been chief of the Soviet space program for 10 years. During that time, he had run the show, directing launches, scheduling maintenance, and selecting cosmonauts for their assignments. Apparently beloved by his cosmonauts, Korolev nevertheless had a sharp temper and little

Known simply as the "Chief Designer," Sergei Korolev was the leader of the Soviet space program from the early 1950s until his death in January 1966. Pictured here is a procession of mourners heading toward Moscow's Red Square at Korolev's funeral.

patience. No wonder: He had no help in the massive job of coordinating the entire space program.

Korolev was in poor health by the end of 1965 and the situation was about to get worse. Diagnosed with polyps in his colon, he was taken in for surgery by a doctor who did not take into account the damage done to his heart by strain and overwork. Korolev died in the hospital, just two days after his fifty-ninth birthday.

Prior to his death, Korolev had never been given full praise and credit for his remarkable role in the Soviet space program. He had been called the "Chief Designer" in the Soviet press, never having his actual name printed. That finally changed in 1966, when he received a state funeral in Moscow.

Leonid Brezhnev, one of the leaders of the collective government, was the highest-ranking official at the funeral. All the scientists, technicians, and dignitaries involved with the space program were there, including Yuri Gagarin who had been Korolev's star pupil back in 1961. There were a number of speakers, with the best, Gagarin, saved for last. In Korolev's eulogy, Gagarin said:

> The name of Sergei Pavlovich [Korolev] is linked with a whole epoch in the history of mankind—the first flights of the artificial Earth satellites, the first flights to the moon and to the planets, the first flights by human beings in space, and the first emergence of a human being into free space.[21]

YURI GAGARIN

Russians learned too late of the greatness of Sergei Korolev, but this was not the case with their next great tragedy. Yuri Gagarin died in 1967. Only six years had passed since Gagarin had been the first man in space, but Soviet officials had not treated him well. Initially, Gagarin had been fussed over and praised, but he had not had the opportunity he really wanted—to go back into space and prove himself once more. His immediate celebrity status after April 1961 meant that Khrushchev and other Russian leaders wanted him grounded, to stay safe so he could trumpet the triumphs of the Soviet space program. Gagarin rapidly tired of cutting ribbons and giving speeches, but there was no alternative. Who was he to defy the Communist Party leaders?

Gagarin died in a plane flight. He was the pilot, and there was some talk that he had been drinking, but history will never know the full truth.

The Russian leaders had gone to great lengths for Korolev's funeral, but they pulled out even more stops for Gagarin. He had a state funeral and was buried not far from his former boss. Several U.S. astronauts requested to come to Russia for the funeral, but their requests were denied. Gagarin's death, the Soviets said, was a purely internal affair.

The Soviet space program was going through a difficult period. The Americans were very conscious that they had enjoyed good luck so far, and just as aware that it could come to an end at any time.

APOLLO BEGINS

The *Mercury* mission had brought the Americans off their planet and into orbit. *Gemini* had shown that ships could rendezvous in space and that men could walk outside their vehicles. *Apollo* was intended to bring men to the moon.

At the beginning of 1967, the U.S. space program was in the best shape ever. Only nine and a half years had passed since the Russians launched *Sputnik*; in the time since then, the Americans had definitely gained the lead in the space race. The directors at NASA did not know that the Russians were in bad shape—even worse with the death of Korolev—but they could feel that the United States had taken the lead. The first *Apollo* mission was scheduled for early 1967.

As mentioned in Chapter 5, President Johnson was never as eager a space enthusiast as President Kennedy. By the beginning of 1967, the United States was involved in the Vietnam War, which had begun in a small way during the Eisenhower and Kennedy administrations, and then grew to giant proportions during Johnson's leadership. By 1967, there were more than a million Americans in South Vietnam, and, despite their overwhelming technical and material superiority, the Americans were not winning the war. As the public became disenchanted with President Johnson and the war, many American youth also began to complain about their country's space program. What could justify the expense of billions of dollars when many Americans were fighting and dying in Vietnam and there was poverty in the United States?

A generational separation had begun. The young people who protested the Vietnam War and the expenses of the space program were in their late teens and early twenties. As the sons and daughters of men and women who had come of age during World War II, this new generation knew little of their parents' sacrifice or fear during previous wars. Quite a few young people believed that the entire conflict between the USSR and the United States—the cold war, space race, and all the rest—was a manufactured crisis designed to enrich the arms manufacturers.

The astronauts observed the protests and confusions, but generally did not experience them directly. The 30 astronauts selected between 1959 and 1964 were almost all of a "middle" generation, neatly sandwiched between the World War II parents and the 1960s children. Most of the astronauts had been born around 1930 and had come of age just after World War II and during the Korean War. They had married sometime in the 1950s, and their children were younger than the generation of protestors of the 1960s. Few of the astronauts commented on the youth rebellion of the 1960s; they were all too busy trying to launch *Apollo* and get to the moon. But the protests were there all the same. Some of the astronauts would have to reckon with the social changes after the fact.

THE WORST DAY

January 27, 1967, was a good day for conducting tests in the new *Apollo* spacecraft. Powered by the *Saturn V* rocket, *Apollo* was expected to be able to reach the moon. Three astronauts climbed the steel bridge up to the spacecraft and entered the space capsule for tests on the ground. Virgil Grissom was one of the original Mercury Seven, Ed White was from the second group, and Roger Chaffee was from the third group.

This was supposed to be a day of routine tests, to make sure all was well with the rocket and capsule. But early that morning, the Houston flight directors heard some terrifying sounds:

On January 27, 1967, tragedy struck the Apollo program when a fire broke out during a launchpad test in one of the command modules. Astronauts Virgil I. Grissom, Edward H. White, and Roger B. Chaffee were killed in the fire. Pictured here is the charred interior of the spacecraft.

> Fire!
> We've got a fire in the cockpit!
> We've got a bad fire . . . get us out. We're burning up.[22]

All efforts came too late. The three brave astronauts perished in the smoke and flames that engulfed their capsule. Many tests and countertests were done, but it all came down to something fairly simple. A spark somewhere in the capsule's wiring created a fire that quickly spread due to the pure oxygen within the capsule.

The Funerals

Americans had experienced setbacks before, but not a defeat and loss like this. Charles A. Bassett, a member of the third group of NASA astronauts, and Elliott M. See had died in a plane crash near St. Louis, Missouri, in February 1966, but their flight had not been connected to Houston, Cape Canaveral, or anything close to it. The loss of the three astronauts of *Apollo I* was devastating.

President Johnson attended the funerals of Chaffee and Grissom at Arlington National Cemetery in Virginia. Observers noted that the families were quite cool to the president, since they blamed him for sending the three men into harm's way. Their grief and anger were understandable, but the president had little to do with such decisions. He was far more occupied with the Vietnam War, with mounting budget deficits, and the youth rebellion that was threatening to topple his presidency.

Time pondered the situation:

> Though it happened under circumstances that, theoretically, are no more hazardous than the car ride to the Cape, the fact that Grissom, White, and Chaffee lost their lives on the ground has a symbolism all its own. For even more important than the down-played dedication, the casual-seeming courage, and the nonchalance under pressure that the astronauts bring to bear in actual flight is the drilled-in professionalism, perfectionism, and thoroughness that they must have to master the incredibly intricate tools of their trade. They are heroic pioneers, but they are also brilliant technicians—and they could not be astronauts without being both.[23]

RECOVERY

NASA and mission control vowed not to send any more men into space until they had worked out the "bugs" from the

OIL, GAS, AND OTHER FUELS

While it is seldom cited as a reason for the current decline of the space program, energy conservation has played a role behind the scenes. In 1967, when the *Saturn* rocket first appeared at Cape Canaveral, Americans bought gasoline for as little as 25 cents a gallon. There was a tremendous supply of oil coming into the country from places as far away as Venezuela and Saudi Arabia. Americans drove large, heavy cars that sometimes got as little as 12 miles to the gallon. No one complained, because fuel expense was one of the lighter aspects of the American family budget.

Then came 1973. In October 1973, Israel and its Arab neighbors fought a two-week conflict called the Yom Kippur War. Neither side really "won" the war, but the oil-rich Arab nations decided to punish the United States and other Western nations for their support of Israel. Gasoline prices doubled in 1974 and did so again in 1979.

Suddenly, Americans experienced a reduction in oil supplies and higher prices. Many alternative types of energy were discussed and even introduced, but neither solar fuel cells nor nuclear reactor energy seemed practical. Then, as the income of average Americans rose during the 1980s and 1990s, they tended to forget the higher oil prices. Although gas was sometimes as high as $1.50 a gallon, Americans could afford it.

Then, in September 2005, Hurricane Katrina slammed into America's Gulf Coast, wrecking large parts of New Orleans and disrupting supplies of oil and natural gas. On some days that autumn, gas at the pump cost as much as $3.50 per gallon. Americans who strained to fill their cars, SUVs, and trucks could not imagine that their government would freely spend valuable fuel trying to go to the moon, Mars, or anywhere else, at least not until a new and cheaper form of energy was found.

system. As luck would have it, they had a major head start. Ever since President Kennedy had expressed the nation's desire to go to the moon before the decade was out, German rocket scientist Wernher von Braun and his group of technicians in Alabama had been working on what became the giant of the age: the *Saturn* rocket. Mission control director Chris Kraft later described the strength of *Saturn*, the most powerful rocket ever devised:

> Wernher von Braun built a masterpiece. Its statistics should never be forgotten.
>
> The first stage was thirty-three feet in diameter. It had five rocket engines, each producing 1.5 million pounds of thrust. Those engines would burn 4.5 million pounds of kerosene and liquid oxygen in just 160 seconds.
>
> The second stage was thirty feet in diameter. It was powered by five slightly smaller rocket engines that burned 1 million pounds of hydrogen and oxygen in the next six and a half minutes after staging.
>
> The third stage sat atop a tapered adapter and was almost twenty-two feet across. This was the S-IVB with one J-2 engine, and it had to be fired twice, once to get the spacecraft—CSM and LM—into Earth orbit, then again to power them away from Earth and toward the moon. Its tanks carried 192,495 pounds of liquid oxygen and 39,735 pounds of liquid hydrogen. Put all three stages together and those numbers still boggle the mind.[24]

Saved by
Saint Nick

Russians and Americans alike faced great challenges in 1968. At times during that difficult year, it seemed as if the world was ending. The war in Vietnam continued with no end in sight. Domestic opposition to the war continued to grow, and in January 1968, Senator Eugene McCarthy announced that he would challenge President Johnson for the Democratic Party nomination in the upcoming presidential election.

Johnson had inherited President Kennedy's policy makers and his agenda. One could say Johnson had even gone beyond Kennedy in promoting his social programs, especially the War on Poverty. But Johnson had allowed himself to be sucked ever deeper into the Vietnam War. Whether Kennedy would have done the same will forever remain open to question. No one expected that McCarthy could unseat a sitting president, but he did just that. When the New Hampshire primary was held in March, McCarthy won enough votes to make Johnson look like a poor candidate, and days later Johnson pulled out of the race for good.

Then another event shook the nation. Just days after the primary, on April 4, 1968, civil rights leader Dr. Martin Luther King Jr., was shot and killed in Memphis, Tennessee. The civil rights movement might be said to have paralleled the space program, in that they began around the same time and ran on parallel tracks. Like two trains headed in the same direction but on different sets of rails, the civil rights movement and the race for space did not intersect. There were no astronauts involved in the civil rights movement, and there were no major civil rights leaders who attached themselves to the space program. Even so, the assassination of a person as great as King could not fail to have an effect on everyone.

At about the same time that King was shot and killed, Senator Robert Kennedy of New York State announced his candidacy for the Democratic presidential nomination. A younger brother of John F. Kennedy (there were four sons in the family), Robert Kennedy was seen as the obvious heir to his brother's legacy throughout the Johnson administration. Now he threw his hat into the ring.

The political battle between McCarthy and Kennedy was one of the most interesting in American politics. Calm, quiet, even retiring by nature, McCarthy was passionately opposed to the Vietnam War, and he drew great applause from youth groups, especially on college campuses. Kennedy did not have as strong a draw with American youth, but he seemed to personify many of the Democratic Party traditions. Shorter and less gregarious than his brother, Robert Kennedy nevertheless emerged as the candidate for 1968. He seemed to have more energy than McCarthy, and a greater chance of winning the general election that fall.

But then Kennedy was shot and killed in Los Angeles on June 6, 1968, just two short months after the death of Martin

Luther King. It seemed that political and social upheaval in the country could not get any worse. But they did. The Democratic National Convention, held in Chicago that summer, was a bitterly contested fight between the supporters of McCarthy and supporters of another candidate, the vice president at the time, Hubert Humphrey. Younger people disliked Humphrey for having supported the Vietnam War. And many people had just plain given up on politics after Kennedy's assassination. There were fights between the Chicago police and protestors, and the Democratic Party emerged in shambles.

The general election that autumn was something of a letdown. The Democrats did nominate Hubert Humphrey. He did his best, but could not distance himself from the policies of Lyndon Johnson and the Vietnam War. The Republicans nominated Richard Nixon of California.

Nixon engineered what must be considered one of the great political comebacks of American political history. Having been narrowly defeated by Kennedy in the presidential election of 1960, Nixon was solidly beaten by Pat Brown in the race for governor of California in 1962. Telling journalists that "you won't have Richard Nixon to kick around anymore," Nixon had gone off into a vengeful retirement. But he had not given up.

Only eight years had passed since the election of 1960, but some people felt as if a lifetime had gone by. In 1960, the country had been rather "plain and square" in that most people claimed to be Republican or Democrat, most said they went to one church or another, and most hoped to work for a corporation some day. Not so in 1968. The youth movement had begun gaining strength in 1965 and had grown by leaps and bounds ever since. Many young people told their dismayed parents that they were dropping out of college, or were going to walk across Asia, or some other equally dramatic thing. Young people then—those who were born in the 1940s—seemed to have very different ideals and goals from their parents. A generation gap truly appeared during the late 1960s.

In November 1968, Richard Nixon was elected the thirty-seventh president of the United States. Pictured here with Lyndon B. Johnson, Nixon was president during all the U.S. moon landings and was instrumental in the development of the space shuttle program.

Young people were especially saddened and disillusioned by the deaths of King and Robert Kennedy. Many said there was no real difference between Hubert Humphrey and Richard Nixon, and so they chose not to vote. That helped Nixon win by a narrow margin in November. After a long period in the political wilderness, Nixon became the nation's thirty-seventh president.

SPACE TO THE RESCUE

If they were looking for good news, Americans found none in the summer of 1968. But that autumn, some Americans returned to something that had previously caught their interest: space.

The deaths of three astronauts in 1967 and the passage of nearly a year and a half of time had led many Americans to forget about the space program. But in the fall of 1968, they learned that NASA was about to launch its most ambitious venture yet: a manned orbit of the moon.

LAST OF THE MERCURY GROUP

By 1968, the year the *Saturn* rocket was ready, most of the original Mercury Seven astronauts had left the scene. Only one man was there to experience all three of the great missions of the early U.S. space program.

John Glenn retired soon after his famous Earth orbit in 1962. Alan Shepard was grounded by an infection of the inner ear (which would later be cured). Donald Slayton had been grounded even earlier and had become taskmaster for all the astronauts. Virgil Grissom had died in a fire in January 1967 and both Gordon Cooper and M. Scott Carpenter had left the space program. That left Walter (Wally) Schirra.

He had always been the noisiest and most playful of the group. Back in 1959, when he first met the press, Schirra, along with Glenn, had raised two hands instead of one, affirming that they would make it into space and also return. Now, in 1968, Schirra had his biggest chance.

The "Wally Schirra" show, as some called it, was not a pleasant flight. Schirra's nerves were on edge, and he and his two fellow crewmen directly disobeyed several orders from mission control. When they returned to Houston, Texas, Schirra went straight to Flight Director Chris Kraft and asked if they were still on speaking terms. Apparently they were, but this was definitely Schirra's last mission.

No matter. Schirra holds the unique distinction of being the only person to have flown in all three phases of the 1960s space program: Mercury, Gemini, and Apollo.

Russians and Americans had both sent unmanned probes to the moon, but a manned flight was something else entirely. It was only seven and a half years since Alan Shepard had flown the first *Mercury* flight, and the little capsule he went up in would fit three or four times in the spacious vehicle planned for the moon mission. Jim Lovell, Frank Borman, and William Anders were the astronauts selected for the mission.

NASA laid its plans well, but late in the process it discovered a major flaw. As was customary, the astronauts would take off into space and then return by touching down somewhere in the Pacific Ocean. But the U.S. Pacific Fleet had already made its plans for the early winter of 1968, and most sailors were going to be at home on leave. These young sailors were operating at a time of war in Vietnam, and giving them an occasional vacation was of great importance to the morale of the fleet as a whole.

Making matters worse, Pacific Force Commander John McCain Jr., had a son, John McCain III (who would later become a U.S. senator), who had recently been captured by the North Vietnamese. Commander McCain might have assumed that he could not change the leave rotation of the Pacific Fleet. But he did so anyway. In one of the truly enlightened moves, of which many were needed for the space program to succeed, McCain gave his full support to the mission. And unlike some commanders who leave all the trouble to others, Commander McCain would be part of the space crew's rescue mission.

McCain's patriotism made the launch possible. Now the question was, could NASA pull it off?

CHRISTMAS WEEK, 1968

The astronauts were in a high state of readiness. Mission control was ready with the microphones, radio, and telemetry. The biggest questions revolved around the *Saturn* rocket (which had never delivered a manned ship) and the delicate rendezvous that would have to be pulled off in Earth's orbit. The crew blasted off on December 21, 1968.

FIFTY CENTS *   DECEMBER 6, 1968

TIME

RACE FOR THE MOON

In anticipation of the race to the moon, *Time*'s December 6, 1968, cover featured a Russian cosmonaut and an American astronaut competing to be first to walk on the moon. The United States would ultimately win the race, as astronaut Neil Armstrong became the first man to walk on the moon on July 20, 1969.

Time magazine ran a cover that showed a Russian cosmonaut and an American astronaut doing a "run" in space for the moon. The truth is that the Russians were well out of the game by this point. They had done quite well in the early stages, but their orbits of 1961 and 1962 had not led to further technical development. One might even say that some of the early American failures turned out to be beneficial, because they instilled a sense of responsibility and determination to make the space program successful.[25]

Lovell, Borman, and Anders worked together like synchronized clocks. Within hours of launching, they had performed a technical feat, detaching the command module from the *Saturn* rocket and then reengaging with the *Saturn*

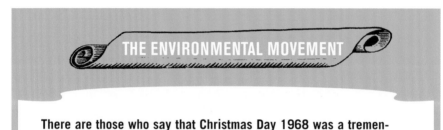

THE ENVIRONMENTAL MOVEMENT

There are those who say that Christmas Day 1968 was a tremendous moment in human history. For the first time ever, humans were able to witness the fragility of their home planet, which could only be done by looking from outer space. Millions of people watched the camera footage on the news or read the essays in *Time*. Many of them were persuaded that more needed to be done to save this planet before humans proceeded elsewhere in the universe.

The environmental movement had begun a few years earlier. Many historians credit Rachel Carson's book *Silent Spring* with launching the movement. Published in 1962, *Silent Spring* predicted that men and women would hear no birds in the future if pesticides continued to be used in farming and gardening.

For the crew of *Apollo VIII*, seeing the earth from space was another huge moment in the growing environmental movement. The very first Earth Day was commemorated in April 1970. Many observers credited the space program, and its pictures of earth from space, with helping to start the movement. The use of advanced technologies has led many people to come to appreciate the beauty and simplicity of the land, earth, and sky that make our planet so beautiful.

Although the moon turned out to be barren and devoid of life, astronauts were not disappointed with their lunar adventures. Sites such as this earthrise, taken during the *Apollo VIII* mission in December 1968, thrilled both the astronauts and the American public.

to "link up" with the lunar module. This would have been unthinkable four years before, but the effort put in by those who worked for NASA helped perfect the difficult rendez-vous maneuver.

Once this was accomplished, it was off to the moon. The astronauts moved through space in a revolving trajectory, meaning that the command module and lunar module orbited around each other as they flew to the moon. Lovell, Borman, and Anders were the first human beings ever to leave the earth's orbit, and a few hours later, they became the first to ever feel themselves "caught" by the orbit of the moon. The last quarter of the ride was rather like "falling" to the moon.

The mission proceeded like clockwork. The men in mission control had continuous voice communication with the three astronauts, whose vital signs were holding steady. But everyone, from the astronauts to the people at mission control, were astonished at what they saw next.

Men and women have watched the sun and the moon for hundreds of thousands of years. Untold generations of humans have admired the blazing heat produced by the sun and the nighttime solace provided by the moon, but not a single person had ever experienced an earthrise until December 24, 1968. On that morning, the three astronauts looked across the lunar surface and saw the earth rise over the moon's horizon. There was nothing like it. There was nothing to which it could be compared. The three astronauts were there to see and orbit the moon, but they were most struck by the earth. It was so blue, so green, and so fragile looking. Its atmosphere could hardly be seen from space, but it was evident that the earth was not like Jupiter or Mars. This planet was filled with life.

Lovell, Borman, and Anders proceeded to orbit the moon. They went around it a total of 11 times, with each orbit taking a couple hours. They saw many astonishing and wonderful sights, but absolutely no signs of life. The moon was barren.

The people at mission control had their most frightening moments on the first orbit. As the command module passed around the dark side of the moon, the side which is never seen from Earth, the command module was out of radio contact for as long as 17 minutes. But then Lovell's voice came on the radio, assuring the people back home that *Apollo VIII* was doing just fine.

The return home was anticlimactic compared to the outbound flight. Lovell, Borman, and Anders crashed down in the Pacific Ocean on December 28, having spent seven days on one of the most incredible rides ever known in human history. *Time* named the three astronauts "Men of the Year." A *Time* editorial mused on the connections and the differences between the youth rebellion of the 1960s and the space program:

> What the rebels and dissenters ask will not be found on the moon: social justice, peace, an end to hypocrisy—in short, Utopia. But to the extent that the rebels really want a new kind of tomorrow—rather than simply a curse on and an escape from today—the moon flight of *Apollo 8* shows how that Utopian tomorrow could come about. For this is what Westernized man can do. He will not turn into a passive, contemplative being; he will not drop out and turn off; he will not seek stability and inner peace in the quest for nirvana. Western man is Faust and if he knows anything at all he knows how to challenge nature, how to dare against dangerous odds and even against reason. He knows how to reach for the moon.[26]

One Giant Leap

Americans went wild over the photos brought back by *Apollo VIII*. Prior to that, the country had begun to show signs of weariness with the space program—its expense, especially. With the arrival of the photos in the beginning of 1969, Americans approached the idea of space with a new verve and vigor; they believed it was possible to do what President Kennedy had promised—to reach the moon before the decade came to an end.

RECOVERY FROM 1968

To put the achievement of a moonwalk in perspective, it is important to look back on where the country stood at the time. The year 1968 had been one of the truly traumatic years in all of American history. Two important leaders had been assassinated; the Democratic National Convention had been little short of a disaster; and many feared that the seams of American life were coming apart. How had it all happened so fast?

Often what seems fast is really slow, when examined under the microscope of history. But 1968 was one of the great exceptions to that rule. The tidal wave of social change that swept the United States between 1965 and 1969 was truly unprecedented. In four short years, the time between when a pupil enters his or her freshman year and graduates from high school, America had changed. Younger people railed against the "system." Older people railed against the irresponsibility of the young. Middle-aged parents were appalled at the sudden change. How could their children, who had been so sweet and complacent in 1965, have become so aggressive by 1969?

The answer is, of course, the Vietnam War. It divided the United States like no other conflict, before or since. By 1969, the United States was truly divided between those who supported the war and those who would do almost anything to stop it. The Vietnam War and the race for space were both products of the 10 years preceding 1969. In both cases, Dwight Eisenhower had laid the early groundwork, and John F. Kennedy had plunged the country headfirst into the cause. In both cases, Lyndon B. Johnson saw no choice but to continue what had been started. But this was not the case with Richard M. Nixon.

Richard Nixon was inaugurated as president on January 20, 1969. Thousands of young people protested the inauguration, saying that Nixon would continue America's downward spiral. Perhaps Nixon did want to remove U.S. troops from Vietnam, but he also felt the time was not right. To leave suddenly would seem like an admission of defeat, and that was something no American president in the 1950s or 1960s was willing to acknowledge. But there was an area in which Nixon could truly shine, with little cost to his administration or his policies. He could back the race for space and bask in the glory of what had been started 10 years ago.

THE CREW OF *APOLLO XI*

The next step in the space program was a mission to walk on the moon. Three men were chosen for this mission, including Neil A. Armstrong, who was selected commander for the flight. Born in Ohio in 1930, he had lived in a large number of small towns, because his father, a military man, was often transferred, and naturally brought his family with him. Armstrong had been an ace pilot for the U.S. Navy and was a test pilot before being chosen for the second group of astronauts in 1962. Known as cool and courageous, Armstrong was an easy choice as commander.

Edwin Eugene Aldrin (he later changed his legal name to "Buzz") was second in command. Born in New Jersey in 1930, Aldrin was the son of a highly educated and highly competitive man, who drove his son in the endless pursuit of excellence. Aldrin graduated third in his class at the United States Military Academy at West Point and was a fighter pilot in the Korean War. He earned a doctorate from the Massachusetts Institute of Technology before becoming a member of the third group of astronauts in 1963. Known as bright and capable, he also had a tendency to talk a lot and was sometimes known for stirring up controversy. Some people asked Armstrong if he would have trouble working with Aldrin: His answer was a cool, collected "no."

Michael Collins was pilot for *Apollo XI*. Also born in 1930, he was the son of a U.S. Army general and the nephew of another. Like Armstrong, Collins had moved around a great deal as a young person, and, like Armstrong, it did not seem to have harmed him a bit. Like Aldrin, Collins had done an extended space walk in 1966. Everyone agreed that Collins was the easiest to talk with of the three astronauts, the one with the fewest set notions about how things "should be" on the flight.

TRAINING FOR THE FLIGHT

All three men knew that their mission was of paramount importance. John F. Kennedy had pledged that the United

Astronauts Neil Armstrong (left), Michael Collins (center), and Buzz Aldrin (right) were the lucky three selected for the _Apollo XI_ mission. The mission's objective was to perform a manned lunar landing and return safely to Earth.

States would reach the moon by 1970, and President Nixon was committed to fulfilling the promise. There could be no mistakes in this great endeavor.

Gene Kranz, one of the directors of mission control, recalled the endless simulations during preflight training in Houston.

SimSup [Simulation Supervisor] for the descent phase was Dick Koos, who struck me as a quiet young academic. In fact, he was a discharged sergeant from the Army Missile Command at Fort Bliss, Texas.... His external demeanor set you up for his training sessions, which were like a rapier, cutting so cleanly that you did not know you were bleeding until long after the thrust. Koos was a worthy adversary and an excellent choice for training my White Team for the *Apollo 11* landing.[27]

Adversary? Yes, that is how it had to be. In order for this first flight to reach the moon, the men at mission control had to be prepared for just about every possibility.

On July 5, 1969, just 11 days before blastoff, Dick Koos was still not satisfied with the response team of Gene Kranz and the people at mission control. He ran them through an alert code named "1201—Executive overflow—no vacant areas." In this simulation, *Apollo XI's* computer system was overloaded, and might need to dump some items in order to take on new data. It was a relatively new idea in 1969, and Kranz's team did not handle it well, leading to an abort command of the simulated mission. Koos scolded them for the mistake, and Kranz and the team accepted his chastisement. They were committed to carrying out the mission.

THE FLIGHT

Armstrong, Aldrin, and Collins blasted off from Cape Canaveral on July 16, 1969. Thousands of people came to watch the mighty boosters lift the rocket into the sky. In no time at all, *Apollo XI* had come into a safe orbit hundreds of miles above the surface of the earth. But that was the easy part. Something much harder was about to be attempted.

Collins had the difficult job of separating the command module from the *Saturn* rocket, sinking behind the *Saturn* rocket, and then linking up with the lunar module. This endeavor had to be done carefully, for the lunar module was too soft and fragile to be carried in the front part of the rocket along with the command module. Collins did the job with no

On July 16, 1969, the *Apollo XI* mission took off from Florida's Kennedy Space Center. Approximately one million people watched the launch outside the space center and another 600 million saw it on television.

problem. When one thinks of the numerous errors and failures of the U.S. space program in the late 1950s, it seems incredible that complicated maneuvers like separation, docking, and taking off could be done so easily. But American scientists, engineers, and physicists had perfected their craft during the 1960s, and U.S. astronauts were trained well for all the programs needed for this great flight.

Soon they were on their way to the moon. The three astronauts of *Apollo XI* were only the second group ever (Jim Lovell's group was the first) to escape Earth's gravity and head for other orbits. Like their predecessors on *Apollo VIII*, the men of *Apollo XI* felt that subtle change as they coasted out of Earth's gravity and began falling into the moon's gravitational pull.

The spacecraft moved straight ahead at times, but there were also times when it revolved as it moved; this was to prevent one side of the craft from becoming too warm because it faced the sun, or too cold because it faced away. The three astronauts soon set up a camera for what would be live broadcasts to Houston's mission control.

As the spacecraft neared the moon, the three astronauts separated. Armstrong and Aldrin floated into the lunar module, while Collins remained in the command module. The sequence and separation had been planned ahead of time. Collins would orbit the moon in the command module while Armstrong and Aldrin would bring the landing module down to the surface of the moon. None of this had ever been done before. Only three men had ever orbited the moon before, and none had landed on the lunar surface.

Armstrong and Aldrin gently separated their module from the command module, and began their historic descent. The lunar module was designed so that the two men were standing upright, using armrests, and looking straight down past their feet, through windows, at the surface of the moon. This was tricky, because they could not be sure whether the surface below them was smooth and even, or whether it was covered with craters. The difference could mean life or death.

The lunar module was extremely lightweight and soft in composition. The astronauts later said they could have poked a hole in it with a penknife. This lightweight composition was just what was needed for the lunar module, but it did not guarantee the astronauts' safety.

As they came within a few miles of the lunar surface, Armstrong radioed back to Earth that there was a blinking light on his console. When asked what kind of warning this was, he replied that it was "Warning 1201." This was exactly the warning that had caused such commotion at mission control during a simulation 10 days earlier. Because of that run-through, and because of the chastisement they had received from the simulation supervisor, Dick Koos, Gene Kranz and his team were able to give a quick "You are Go" back to Armstrong. One major hurdle was passed, and the descent continued.[28] Armstrong and Aldrin were in constant contact with mission control, which in turn was in constant contact with CBS News in New York City. The American public was finding out what was going on just moments after it had occurred.

Then there was a second alarm. This one had to do with the fuel in the lunar module, called *Eagle*. In order to keep the module light, NASA engineers had designed it with just a small pack of fuel. Armstrong and Aldrin were down to only a small amount of fuel left in their tank when they landed on the moon. But then Armstrong sent off a message: "Houston, Tranquility Base here. The Eagle has landed."[29]

It was hard to believe. People at mission control went crazy with jubilation. Walter Cronkite and Walter Schirra, who were relaying information to the American public on CBS, were as stunned and amazed as their listeners. The Americans had done it. They had fulfilled Kennedy's pledge to land on the moon.

But the astronauts had not yet walked on the lunar surface. Three hours passed before that would happen. In that time, Armstrong and Aldrin made their final preparations. Long before, it had been decided that Armstrong would be the first man on the moon and that Aldrin would be second. This decision had required changing established protocol, which was that the commander of a spacecraft should exit second or last from his ship. But the people at mission control had decided that they wanted the cool, collected Armstrong to be first.

Viewers around the world watched as the hatch opened. Out stepped Armstrong, with his head turned back to the module and his feet very slowly moving down the ladder. He had to be careful for so many reasons. A hasty move could rip something, either on his space suit or on the lunar module. As his foot moved from the last ladder rung to the lunar surface,

CRONKITE AND SCHIRRA

As *Apollo XI* neared the moon, Walter Cronkite, the longtime anchor of the CBS Evening News, went on air with astronaut Walter Schirra. They made an unusual team. Cronkite looked the image of a sun-beaten reporter, and he had the serious, yet kindly, manner that made him famous throughout the world. Schirra was still the irrepressible young man who had been selected as one of the Mercury Seven back in 1959.

Cronkite had seven notebooks crammed with information about space and the mission to the moon, and yet he managed to appear anecdotal and comfortable with the subject. Schirra chatted with Cronkite; the two men discussed complex subjects with ease.

As *Apollo XI* neared the lunar surface, the atmosphere became more tense, both at mission control and at CBS News headquarters. CBS decided to do a live broadcast of the entire lunar landing, making for the longest single program in the network's history.

For millions of TV viewers, the voices of Walter Cronkite and Walter Schirra would be among their lasting memories of those tense moments as *Apollo XI* prepared for the hardest part of its mission.

Armstrong uttered his famous words: "That's one small step for man, one giant leap for mankind."[30]

People on Earth were delirious with joy.

Cronkite had narrated the news events of President Kennedy's assassination and the tumultuous Democratic National Convention riots of 1968. One suspects he had longed for a moment like this, a moment of sheer joy, of good news. He announced to the eager viewers: "Armstrong is on the moon! Neil Armstrong, a 38-year-old American, standing on the surface of the moon! On this July twentieth, nineteen hundred and sixty-nine."[31] Cronkite did not weep, but his eyes were moist. So were the eyes of millions of people around the world. For a few precious minutes, hours even, no one talked about the "American" achievement. Instead this was a human achievement, the first time the small hands and feet of humans had reached another surface in space.

Aldrin came out a few minutes later. For a time, the two men cavorted on the lunar surface. They took photos, scooped up small soil samples, and planted a plaque that stated they came in peace for all mankind. These were moments that became embedded in the memories of millions. Yet, one wonders, how was Michael Collins doing?

Collins was in the command module orbiting the moon. He orbited it every two hours, and came very close to passing right over the landing site, but he never quite made out his two comrades on the lunar surface. Collins certainly had the loneliest job of the three. But when asked about it years later, he chose not to focus on that. His great fear, he said, was that something would go wrong, that Armstrong and Aldrin would be marooned, and that he would have to travel back to Earth alone.

After a brief stay on the moon's surface, Armstrong and Aldrin were ready to lift off once more. They had only spent a couple hours outside the space capsule; now it was time to see if the lunar module could do one last great and important job.

On July 20, 1969, Neil Armstrong and Buzz Aldrin became the first humans to walk on the moon. The duo spent more than two and half hours on the moon's surface, and Armstrong took this famous photo of Aldrin shortly before they returned to their capsule.

The lunar module fired up and blasted off, carrying the two men back into orbit, where they were able to link up with Collins. The rest was easy. *Apollo XI* headed back to Earth. The three astronauts survived the fiery ordeal of reentry to the earth's atmosphere, and plunged down into the Pacific Ocean. President Nixon was waiting aboard the USS *Hornet*.

Space in the Imagination

The 1969 landing on the moon was one of the great events of human history. For a few precious minutes or hours, men and women throughout the world looked with awe, both at the power of the natural world, and at the increasing ability of humans to find their way through it.

Popular culture echoed the accomplishments that were happening in technology and science. The late 1960s and early 1970s witnessed a burgeoning of new programs about space and man's attempts to "conquer" it. There was the ever-popular television series *Lost in Space*. There was *Star Trek*, with its assertion that Captain Kirk and his spaceship would go where no man had gone before. And, looming above all the others, there was *2001: A Space Odyssey*. The film came out in 1968 to rave reviews. Americans flocked to see this vision of the future, in which human technology clashed with primitive human emotions. Most compelling was the computer named Hal, who continually informed the astronauts of the statistics and probabilities of any event. Americans wondered if this was the future that travel to outer space would bring. And as they wondered, their world kept changing.

VIETNAM AND WATERGATE

As discussed previously, President Nixon had pulled off one of the truly great comebacks in political history, winning the presidential election of 1968. Nixon seemed to have many advantages that year. But he continued to be plagued by the war in Vietnam.

The race for space, the civil rights movement, and the Vietnam War were all happening at roughly the same time, and though the movements were distinct and separate from each other, jointly they seemed to herald a new age and time. At the beginning of the decade, Americans were thrilled by the race for space, ambivalent (at first) about the civil rights movement, and supportive of the war in Vietnam (at first). By 1970, however, attitudes had changed. By then, a majority of Americans supported the civil rights movement, and a majority were opposed to the continuing war in Vietnam. By the 1970s, the space race seemed to have lost its importance.

Political and military events—rather than scientific ones—claimed the public's attention in the early 1970s. Nixon won a second presidential term in 1972, but he still had not figured out how to get the U.S. military out of Vietnam. The civil rights movement was still pressing forward, but it had been slowed by the death of its greatest leader, Martin Luther King Jr. Space seemed less important than before.

When *Apollo XIII* aimed for the moon just two years after the first landing there, the major news networks did not at first carry the mission live. They later picked up the story when the astronauts ran into serious trouble during the mission. Television producers defended their initial decision by saying that Americans were tired of hearing about space. Historian

President Richard Nixon greets the *Apollo XI* astronauts outside their isolation unit, shortly after they returned to Earth on July 24, 1969. During the meeting, Nixon touted the significance of the mission by stating: "This is the greatest week in the history of the world since Creation."

Marina Benjamin gives one of the more plausible answers as to why this might have been so:

> Although my memory had no doubt squashed together a train of events that unfolded over a sensible period of time, it still seems to me that one day we were marveling at how men walked on the moon and the next we'd forgotten all about it. I didn't understand then about budget cuts and retrenchment, or the allure of executive jobs in finance and industry, and I certainly didn't see how people who'd been figureheads of the most dynamic agency in the world could

be soundlessly absorbed into its bureaucratic ranks. All I knew was that the astronauts had gone.[32]

During 1969, space exploration took center stage in the United States. Perhaps the events of that year, and those of the next few as well, can help to explain why humans did not go farther in their ventures into space. There were several later landings on the moon, but none of them created much excitement. Americans seemed satisfied that their technological superiority had been demonstrated, and missions to the moon lost much of their urgency. This was not how NASA intended it to be. The scientists, engineers, and flight controllers believed that a moon landing was a great first step, one that would lead Americans to even greater accomplishments. Some people confidently predicted that Americans would next land on Mars.

But this would not be accomplished right away. All it takes is one simple calculation and comparison. The moon is about 239,000 miles (384,635 kilometers) from Earth. Mars is 22.5 million miles (36.2 million kilometers) away, nearly 100 times farther in distance. This means that it would take astronauts about a year to travel from earth to Mars, even traveling at the highest speeds imaginable.

And what about the Russians?

Nikita Khrushchev was now dead. The collective leadership that replaced him had been reduced to Leonid Brezhnev, who was just as interested in space as Khrushchev had been. But Brezhnev faced serious economic restraints in the 1970s. The Soviet Union was going broke, and there was much less money for space exploration than in the past. Then, too, Brezhnev wanted to improve relations with the United States and so it did not make sense to inflame tensions with another space race.

The Russian public was as weary of space as were the Americans. The 1970s are now known as a time of quiet unrest in the Soviet Union, a time when many Russians questioned the enormous expenses for the military when average people could

On January 28, 1986, the space shuttle *Challenger* tragically blew up just 73 seconds after take off. All seven crewmembers—Michael J. Smith, Francis Scobee, Ronald McNair, Ellison Onizuka, Christa McAuliffe, Gregory Jarvis, and Judith Resnik—were killed in the disaster.

not obtain a telephone or a car. And so, during this period, the Soviet Union and the United States were equally disinterested in space.

Yet the fascination continued with television programs like *Star Trek* and *Lost in Space*. Americans still had some interest in space, but in an abstract way. Having seen two men land on the moon and describe its surface, they no longer needed to know those technical details. Instead, they were interested in what Mars was like. And how about Jupiter?

Manned flights to these distant places were out of the question. So the U.S. space program turned to unmanned flights, or probes. Like the Russians, NASA learned that the public did not care as much when people were not actually traveling to space. No matter how much data was brought back, the American willingness to fund space exploration continued to decline. Then came the climactic blow.

On January 28, 1986, which happened to be very close to the nineteenth anniversary of the terrible day when Virgil Grissom, Edward White, and Roger Chaffee lost their lives in a capsule fire, NASA sent up the space shuttle *Challenger* from Cape Canaveral. Aboard were seven crewmembers, including Christa McAuliffe, who was to be the first teacher in space. The shuttle exploded just six minutes after takeoff, and all seven died. NASA had moved too fast that day, and had gone ahead even though there was ice on parts of the launching pad. The later investigation revealed bad judgment on NASA's part, which caused many Americans to give up on the space program entirely.

THE FALL OF COMMUNISM

Just three years later, in the autumn of 1989, the Soviet Union stood by and watched as the states that had for a long time made up the union—virtually all of Eastern Europe—overthrew Communist Party rule. By January 1, 1990, almost all the former Communist nations had become independent. The Iron Curtain was no more.

There were many benefits to the end of the Soviet Union and the fall of Communism. American researchers began to learn information about the Soviet space program that had been kept secret for decades. But the space program of the United States took yet another blow. With the demise of the Soviet Union, it no longer seemed necessary to develop a missile shield in space, or even to keep astronauts in space at all. NASA funding continued to drop.

MODERN SPACE EXPLORATION

Those who had been born during the space-race era, roughly from 1957 to 1969, can look back with pride at the accomplishments of men and women in outer space, but those achievements also brought about something unintended. People the world over have come to realize how precious Earth

GLENN'S FINALE

Much of the story of the space race has to do with "comebacks." The Russians were in the lead until 1965, when the Americans came back to forge ahead in the space race. Richard Nixon lost decisively in two elections, but then came back to win the presidential election of 1968. Yet one of the most impressive of all the comebacks belonged to an astronaut.

By 1998, John Glenn had been through one of the most illustrious careers of the twentieth century. The first American to orbit the earth (1962), he had also been the first to pilot a jet at supersonic speed across the United States (1957). He had run for the U.S. Senate, losing twice, but then came back to win in 1974. He served as a Democratic senator for Ohio between 1974 and 1999. There was still one more show.

In 1998, NASA announced that John Glenn would become the oldest man ever to go into space. Glenn was 77 when he spent 10 consecutive days in space in October 1998. A man who had been justly celebrated in Tom Wolfe's book *The Right Stuff*, Glenn had accomplished one more feat. As the twentieth century ended, he was the most recognized of the many astronauts, and the one most enshrined in the public imagination. As Gene Kranz put it: "Glenn was simply an old-fashioned, star-spangled hero. He spoke of God and country and the flag and the bravery of his fellow astronauts, and he actually meant what he said."*

---

* Gene Kranz, *Failure Is Not an Option* (New York: Simon & Schuster, 2000), 77.

is, that there is not—at least on the surface—any other planet that supports life.

The space race was an incredibly exciting time. Millions of people still recall many of these great moments. But the promise of space remains unfulfilled. There are no colonies on Mars, no plants growing in other atmospheres. For the moment, space remains most poignant and most powerful in the imagination, which is where it began, way back when, with writers like Jules Verne and H. G. Wells.

CHRONOLOGY

1865   *From the Earth to the Moon* published in France.

1898   *War of the Worlds* first published in England.

1899   Robert Goddard has his vision of space flight.

1917   Communist revolution overthrows the Russian government.

1921   Soviet Russia becomes Union of Soviet Socialist Republics.

1939   World War II begins.

1945   Wernher von Braun and other German scientists surrender to Americans at the end of World War II.

1946   Cold war between United States and Soviet Union begins.

1953   Joseph Stalin dies in Russia; Dwight Eisenhower becomes president of the United States.

1957   Soviet Union launches *Sputnik.*

1958   On January 31, *Explorer I* becomes first U.S. satellite in space; NASA established in United States.

1959   Mercury Seven astronauts chosen by NASA; Nikita Khrushchev visits the United States; Russian probe captures first photographs of dark side of the moon.

1960   Joseph Kittinger rises in a helium-filled balloon; John F. Kennedy defeats Richard Nixon in presidential election.

1961   Kennedy inaugurated; Yuri Gagarin is the first human in orbit; Alan Shepard goes up in flight; Kennedy and Khrushchev meet in Vienna, Austria.

1962   John Glenn orbits Earth; NASA announces second group of nine astronauts; Cuban Missile Crisis takes place in October.

1963 Kennedy proposes that Russians and Americans collaborate in space; Kennedy is shot and killed in Dallas; Lyndon B. Johnson becomes new U.S. president; NASA selects third astronaut group.

1964 Russians launch *Voshkod I*; Nikita Khrushchev is ousted and replaced by a collective leadership.

1965 Russians are first to walk in space; Americans do the same in *Gemini V* and later perform first rendezvous and docking in space.

1966 Michael Collins performs two space walks.

1967 Three astronauts—Virgil I. Grissom, Ed White, and Roger B. Chaffee—die in the flames of *Apollo I*.

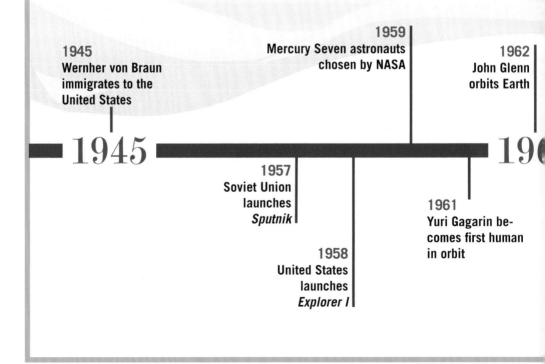

TIMELINE

1945
Wernher von Braun immigrates to the United States

1959
Mercury Seven astronauts chosen by NASA

1962
John Glenn orbits Earth

1945

196

1957
Soviet Union launches *Sputnik*

1961
Yuri Gagarin becomes first human in orbit

1958
United States launches *Explorer I*

1968   Assassinations of Martin Luther King Jr., and Robert
        Kennedy; *Apollo VIII* reaches and orbits the moon.

1969   Richard Nixon inaugurated president; *Apollo XI* takes
        Americans to the moon.

1970   *Apollo XIII* suffers an explosion in its oxygen tanks, but
        astronauts return safely; first Earth Day is celebrated.

1972   Richard Nixon reelected president by a landslide; resigns
        from office two years later following Watergate scandal.

1986   Space shuttle *Challenger* explodes minutes after liftoff.

1989   Former Soviet nations of Eastern Europe throw off
        Communist rule.

1991   Soviet Union ceases to exist; replaced by the
        Russian Federation.

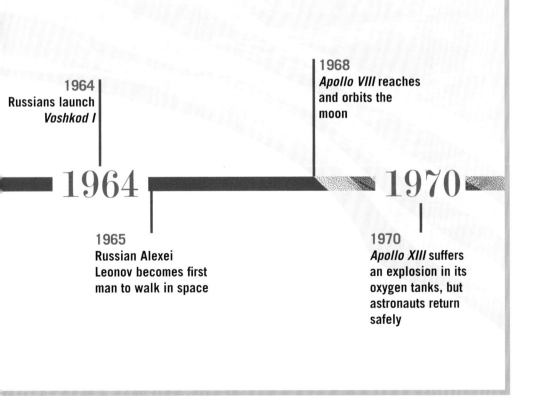

1964
Russians launch
Voshkod I

1968
Apollo VIII reaches
and orbits the
moon

1964

1970

1965
Russian Alexei
Leonov becomes first
man to walk in space

1970
Apollo XIII suffers
an explosion in its
oxygen tanks, but
astronauts return
safely

NOTES

CHAPTER 1

1. Richard L. Witkin, ed., *The Challenge of the Sputniks, in the Words of President Eisenhower and Others* (Garden City, N.Y.: Doubleday, 1958), 19.
2. Ibid., 36.
3. Ibid., 40.
4. William Roy Shelton, *American Space Exploration: The First Decade* (New York: Little Brown and Company, 1960), 41.
5. Ibid., 41–42.
6. Ibid., 42–43.

CHAPTER 2

7. Jules Verne, *From the Earth to the Moon*, English translation New York: P.F. Collier & Sons, 1905), 21.
8. Ibid., 145.
9. Milton Lehman, *This High Man: The Life of Robert H. Goddard* (New York: Farrar, Straus and company, 1963), 26.

CHAPTER 3

10. "Voyage of the Explorer," *Time*, February 10, 1958, 16.
11. Milton Bracker, "Jupiter-C is Used," *New York Times*, February 1, 1958, 1.
12. *The First Man in Space: The Record of Yuri Gagarin's Historic First Vehicle into Cosmic Space* (New York: Crosscurrents Press, 1961), 8–9.
13. Gene Kranz, *Failure Is Not an Option* (New York: Simon & Schuster, 2000), 53.

CHAPTER 4

14. M. Scott Carpenter, et al., *We Seven: By the Astronauts Themselves* (New York: Simon & Schuster, 1962), 289.
15. Ibid., 293.
16. Ibid., 300–301.

CHAPTER 5

17. Chris Kraft, *Flight: My Life in Mission Control* (New York: Dutton, 2001), 213–214.
18. *Time*, June 11, 1965, cover story, 25.
19. James R. Hansen, *First Man: The Life of Neil A. Armstrong* (New York: Simon & Schuster, 2005), 258.
20. Ibid., 265.

CHAPTER 6

21. James Harford, *Korolev: How One Man Masterminded the Soviet Drive to Beat America to the Moon* (Hoboken, N.J.: John Wiley, 1997), 284–285.
22. Kranz, *Failure Is Not an Option*, 197.
23. *Time*, February 3, 1967, cover story, 13.
24. Kraft, *Flight: My Life in Mission Control*, 279.

CHAPTER 7

25. *Time* Cover, December 23, 1968.
26. "Of Revolution and the Moon," essay, *Time*, January 3, 1969, 17.

CHAPTER 8

27. Kranz, *Failure Is Not an Option*, 263.
28. Ibid., 270.
29. Hansen, *First Man: The Life of Neil A. Armstrong*, 458.
30. Ibid., 473.
31. Ibid., 492.

CHAPTER 9

32. Marina Benjamin, *Rocket Dreams: How the Space Age Shaped Our Vision of a World Beyond* (New York: The Free Press, 2003), 29–30.

BIBLIOGRAPHY

Benjamin, Marina. *Rocket Dreams: How the Space Age Shaped Our Vision of a World Beyond.* New York: The Free Press, 2003.

Cassutt, Michael. *Who's Who in Space.* New York: Macmillan, 1999.

Clark, Philip. *The Soviet Manned Space Program.* New York: Orion Books, 1988.

Dickson, Paul. *Sputnik: The Shock of the Century.* New York: Walkerbooks, 2001.

Grimwood, James M. *Project Mercury: A Chronology.* Washington D.C.: NASA Special Publication, 1963.

Hansen, James R. *First Man: The Life of Neil A. Armstrong.* New York: Simon & Schuster, 2005.

Kraft, Chris. *Flight: My Life in Mission Control.* New York: Dutton, 2001.

Kranz, Gene. *Failure Is Not an Option.* New York: Simon & Schuster, 2000.

Launius, Roger D., Robert W. Smith, and John M. Logsdon, eds. *Reconsidering Sputnik: Forty Years since the Soviet Satellite.* Amsterdam, The Netherlands: Harwood Academic Publishers, 2000.

McDougall, Walter A. *The Heavens and the Earth: A Political History of the Space Age.* New York: Basic Books, 1985.

Oberg, James. *Red Star in Orbit: The Inside Story of Soviet Failures and Triumphs in Space.* New York: Random House, 1981.

Witkin, Richard L. ed. *The Challenge of the Sputniks, in the Words of President Eisenhower and Others.* Garden City, N.Y.: Doubleday, 1958.

Wolfe, Tom. *The Right Stuff.* New York: Farrar, Straus & Giroux, 1979.

Further Reading

Benjamin, Marina. *Rocket Dreams: How the Space Age Shaped Our Vision of a World Beyond*. New York: The Free Press, 2003.

Dille, John. *Americans in Space*. New York: HarperCollins, 1965.

Goodyear, Anne Collins, Anthony M. Springer, and Bertram Ulrich, eds. *Flight: A Celebration of 100 Years in Art and Literature*. New York: Welcome Books, 2003.

Kittinger, Joseph W., Jr. "The Long, Lonely Leap." *National Geographic*, December 1960, 854–873.

Kraft, Chris. *Flight: My Life in Mission Control*. New York: Dutton, 2001.

Kranz, Gene. *Failure Is Not an Option*. New York: Simon & Schuster, 2000.

O'Neil, Doris C., ed. *Life: The '60s*. New York: Little, Brown & Company, 1989.

Wolfe, Tom. *The Right Stuff*. New York: Farrar, Straus & Giroux, 1979.

WEB SITES

The First United States Satellite and Space Launch Vehicle

http://history.nasa.gov/sputnik/expinfo.html

Milestones of Flight

http://www.nasm.si.edu/exhibitions/gal100/exp1.html

The Space Race

http://www.nasm.si.edu/exhibitions/gal114/SpaceRace/sec100/sec100.htm

New York Times: Sputnik

http://www.nytimes.com/partners/aol/special/sputnik/

PICTURE CREDITS

INDEX

Agena, 53
Aldrin, Edwin Eugene ("Buzz"),
  76–81, 83–84
Anders, William, 68, 70, 72–73
Apollo program, 14, 57–60, 67
  Apollo I, 60
  Apollo VIII, 70–73, 74, 80
  Apollo XIII, 53, 86
  launchpad test tragedy, 58–60
Apollo XI, 76–84
  command module separation, 80
  crew of, 76
  fight of, 78–84
  launch of, 79
  lunar module *Eagle*, 78,
    80–84
  Saturn rocket for, 78
  training for flight, 76–78
Arlington National Cemetery, 60
Armstrong, Neil
  Agena rendezvous attempt, 53
  Apollo XI mission, 76–84
  famous words of, 81, 83
  first man on moon, 69
  in Gemini Nine, 39, 40
Army Ballistic Missile Agency, 23

Baltimore Gun Club, 13–17
Barbicane, Impey (fictional
  character), 15, 16
Baruch, Bernard, 4
Bassett, Charles A., 60
Benjamin, Marina, 86
Berkner, Lloyd, 3
Blue Team, 51
Borman, Frank, 40, 68, 70, 72–73
Brezhnev, Leonid, 48, 56, 88
Brown, Pat, 65

Cape Canaveral, Florida, 8–10, 16,
  29, 37
capitalist West, 5, 43
Carpenter, Malcolm Scott, 28, 67

Carson, Rachel, 70
Castro, Fidel, 48
Chaffee, Roger, 58–60, 90
Challenger space shuttle, 89, 90
civil rights movement, 64, 86
cold war, 34, 40, 45, 58
Collins, Michael, 76, 77, 78–80, 81
Columbia, 14
Columbiad, 14, 16
command module, 14, 72
Communist government, Soviet
  Union, 19, 48, 90
Conrad, Charles Jr., 40
Cooper, Leroy Gordon Jr., 28, 67
Cosmodrome, 41
cosmonauts, 29–32
  trainer for, 29, 41
  See also individual cosmonauts
Cronkite, Walter, 81, 82, 83
Cuban Missile Crisis, 40–42,
  44, 48

de Gaulle, Charles, 34
Democratic National Convention,
  65, 74–75, 83
Democratic Party, 64–65
Department of Defense, 9
dog orbiting earth, 5–6

Eagle lunar module, 78, 80–81
Earth Day, 70
earthrise, 71, 72
Eisenhower, President Dwight
  ("Ike"), 5–8, 27, 33, 75
energy conservation, 61
environmental movement, 70
Explorer, 8, 25–26
  Explorer I, 26
  Explorer II, 26–327
  Redstone Rocket, 25–26

Freedom VII, 32
Friendship VII, 36–41

From the Earth to the Moon (Verne), 13, 14, 17
fuel conservation, 61

Gagarin, Yuri, 29–32, 47
  death of, 56
  eulogy for Korolev, 56
Geiger counter, 26–27
Gemini Nine astronauts, 39–40
Gemini program, 46, 57, 67
  Gemini IV, 52
  Gemini VI, 53
  Gemini VII, 53
  Gemini III, 50
Gemini IV, 50, 51
generation gap, 65, 75
Germany's V-2 Rocket program, 23–25
Glenn, John H. Jr., 91
  Friendship VII orbit, 36–41
  in Mercury Seven, 28, 29
  retirement of, 67
Goddard, Robert, 19–22
Great Depression, 1
"Great Society" programs, 45
Grissom, Virgil I., 28, 58–60, 67, 90
Guggenheim family, 21
Gulag, 29
Gun Club of Baltimore, 13–17

Harvard College Observatory, 15
heat shield, 38
Hitler's V-2 Rocket program, 23–25
Hodge, John, 51
Houseman, John, 18
Humphrey, Hubert, 65, 66
Hurricane Katrina, 61

International Geophysical Year (IGY), 3, 4
Iron Curtain, 90

Jarvis, Gregory, 89
Jet Propulsion Laboratory, 8, 23
Johnson, Lyndon B., 66
  at astronauts' funerals, 60
  social program supporter, 44, 63
  Vietnam War and, 57, 63, 65, 75

Kaplan, Dr. Joseph, 4
Kazakhstan, 41, 47
Kennedy, Jacqueline, 34
Kennedy, President John F., 57, 63, 65
  assassination, 43, 44, 83
  Cuban Missile Crisis, 40
  man on moon goal, 45, 62, 74, 76, 81
  medal presentation, Glenn, 39
  "summit" with Khrushchev, 33–34
  Vietnam War, 75
Kennedy, Senator Robert, 40, 41, 64, 66
Kennedy Space Center, 79
Khrushchev, Nikita, 29
  in Cuban Missile Crisis, 41
  as new USSR leader, 5
  removal from power, 46
  replaced by Brezhnev, 47–53, 88
  space race goals, 45
  "summit" with President Kennedy, 33–34
  Time's "Man of the Year," 10–12
  women in space propaganda, 43
King, Dr. Martin Luther Jr., 64, 66, 86
Koos, Dick, 77–78, 81
Korean War, 36, 58, 76
Korolev, Sergei, 45
  cosmonaut trainer, 29, 41
  death of, 54–56, 57
Kraft, Chris, 50, 51, 52, 62, 67
Kranz, Gene, 51, 77–78, 91
Kremlin, 5, 12

Laika, first animal in orbit, 5–6
Leave it to Beaver, 3
Lenin, Vladimir, 5
Leonov, Alexei, 49–50
Lindbergh, Charles, 20–21
Lost in Space, 85, 89
Lovell, James Jr., 40, 68, 70, 72–73, 80
lunar landing, 47, 66, 80–84, 88

"Man of the Year," 10–12
Mars, 88, 89, 92

Martians, 17, 18
Marx, Karl, 5
McAuliffe, Christa, 89, 90
McCain, John III, 68
McCain, John Jr., 68
McCarthy, Senator Eugene, 63–64
McDivitt, James A., 40, 50
McNair, Ronald, 89
Mercury program, 57, 67, 68
Mercury Seven astronauts, 28–29,
    32, 67
      earth orbit preparation, 35–36
      test pilot experience, 39, 40
      tragic deaths, former members, 58
mission control, 53, 68, 72, 78, 81
moon
      distance from earth, 16, 88
      See also earthrise; lunar landing

National Aeronautics and Space
    Administration (NASA), 14, 45
      creation of, 27–28
      funding decrease, 90
      moon orbit venture, 67–68
National Science Foundation, 8
Nazi Germany, 34
New Nine astronauts, 40, 50
Newsweek, 29
Newton, Sir Isaac, 19
New York Herald Tribune, 4
New York Times, 3, 4, 20
Nixon, Richard M.
      and *Apollo XI* astronauts, 84, 87
      elected 37th U.S. president, 66,
        75, 91
      man on moon goal, 76–77
      Republican nomination of, 65
      Vietnam War and, 86

Onizuka, Ellison, 89

Paine, Tom, 45
probes, 47, 68, 89

"Race for Space," 3, 43, 75
      beginning of, 12
      modern-day, 90–92
      U.S. catching up in, 49

U.S. lead in, 57
youth movement and, 58
See also space "firsts"
radiation, 26–27
Red Square, 55
Redstone Rocket, 25–326
Red Team, 51
rendezvous, 49, 52–53
Resnick, Judith, 89
Right Stuff, The (Wolfe), 91
rocket. See *Saturn* rocket; V-2 rocket
    program
Russia
      missiles in Communist Cuba, 40
      Moscow's Red Square, 55
      space program budget, 45
      space program decline, 69
      See also Soviet Union

satellite. See *Explorer; Sputnik:
    Vanguard*
Saturn rocket, 61, 67
      for *Apollo XI*, 78
      for manned lunar orbit, 68,
        70–71
      most powerful rocket, 62
      Saturn V, 58
Schirra, Walter M. Jr., 28, 29, 67,
    81, 82
Schooley, Herschel, 9
Scobee, Francis, 89
Scott, Dave, 53
See, Elliott M. Jr., 40
Shepard, Alan B. Jr., 32–33, 35, 37
      first *Mercury* flight, 68
      in Mercury Seven, 28, 67
Silent Spring (Carson), 70
Slayton, Donald K., 28, 33, 67
Smith, Michael J., 89
Smithsonian magazine, 20
social change, 75
socialism, 5
solar radiation, 26–27
Soviet space program
      "Chief Designer," 55–56
      disinterest in, 89
      first satellite in orbit, 3–5
      lack of media coverage, 30

Soviet Union, 3
  Communist government of, 19
  fall of Communism, 90
  unrest in, 88
  See also Russia
space "firsts"
  American in orbit, 32–33
  American space walk, 50–52
  animal to orbit earth, 4–6
  man to orbit earth, 29–32
  satellite, 3–4
  U.S. astronaut to orbit earth,
    36–41
  U.S. satellite, 11
  walk in space, 49–52
  walk on moon, 69, 81–84
  woman in space, 42–43
space race. *See* "Race for Space"
space shuttle *Challenger*, 89, 90
space walks, 49–52
Sputnik, 12, 25, 36, 57
  Sputnik I, 2, 3–4, 5, 23, 26
  Sputnik II, 4–6, 26
Stafford, Thomas P., 40
Stalin, Premier Joseph, 29
Star Trek, 85, 89

Tereshkova, Valentina, 42–43
test pilots, 27, 29, 39, 40, 76
third law of motion, 19
Time magazine, 25, 29, 50, 70
  Apollo I tragedy, 60
  "Man of the Year," 10–12
  "Men of the Year," 73
  "Race for the Moon" cover, 69
Tsiolkovsky, Konstantin, 18–19,
  22, 29
2001: A Space Odyssey, 85

Union of Soviet Socialist Republics
  (USSR). *See* Soviet Union
unmanned craft, 47, 68, 89.
  See also *Sputnik*
U.S. Army, 23–24, 25–26.
  See also *Explorer*
U.S. Navy, 8, 11. See also *Vanguard*

U.S. Pacific Fleet, 68
USS *Hornet*, 84
USS *Lake Champlain*, 33
U.S. space program, 79–80
  budding, 8–9
  disinterest in, 89
USSR. *See* Soviet Union

V-2 rocket program, 23–25
Van Allen, James, 26
Vanguard, 7–10, 25–26
  failed launch attempts, 10, 11
  Vanguard I, 11
  Vanguard TV3, 9–10, 25
Verne, Jules, 13–17, 19, 22, 92
Vietnam War, 57–58, 60, 63, 65, 68
  opposition to, 64, 86
  U.S. divided on, 75
von Braun, Wernher, 23–25
  Saturn rocket, 62
Voshkod, 46
Voshkod II, 47
Vostok, 46
  Vostok I, 30–32, 47
  Vostok VI, 42–43

Walsh, J. Paul, 9
War of the Worlds (Wells), 17, 19–20
  radio show rendition, 18
War on Poverty, 63
Watergate, 86
Webb, James, 45
Wells, H. G., 17, 19, 22, 92
Wells, Orson, 18
White, Edward H. II, 40, 50–52,
  58–60, 90
White Sands Proving Grounds,
  24–25
White Team, 51, 78
Wilson, Charles, 23
Wolfe, Tom, 91
World War II, 34, 58

Yom Kippur War, 61
Young, John W., 40
youth movement, 65, 73

ABOUT THE AUTHOR

SAMUEL WILLARD CROMPTON was born eight weeks after Yuri Gagarin's famous flight and four weeks after Alan Shepard's. He has always felt a sentimental connection to the early days of the space program. Crompton is the author or editor of 40 books, many of them written for Chelsea House. He is also an adjunct professor of history at Holyoke Community College and Westfield State College, both in Massachusetts.